Sushma Rudraswamy
Naganandini Sampath
Nagabhushana Doggalli

Hospital Waste Management Training Among The Staff Of Dental Teaching Hospitals In Bangalore City

Hospital Waste Management

Anchor Academic
Publishing

Rudraswamy, Sushma, Sampath, Naganandini, Doggalli Nagabhushana: Hospital Waste Management Training Among The Staff Of Dental Teaching Hospitals In Bangalore City. Hospital Waste Management, Hamburg, Anchor Academic Publishing 2013

Buch-ISBN: 978-3-95489-154-2
PDF-eBook-ISBN: 978-3-95489-654-7
Druck/Herstellung: Anchor Academic Publishing, Hamburg, 2013

Bibliografische Information der Deutschen Nationalbibliothek:
Die Deutsche Nationalbibliothek verzeichnet diese Publikation in der Deutschen Nationalbibliografie; detaillierte bibliografische Daten sind im Internet über http://dnb.d-nb.de abrufbar.

Hermannstal 119k, 22119 Hamburg
http://www.diplomica-verlag.de, Hamburg 2013
Printed in Germany

ACKNOWLEDGEMENT

It is my privilege and honor to express my most sincere and heartfelt thanks to ***Dr.M R.Shankar Aradhya****, Professor and Head, Department of Preventive and Community Dentistry, Oxford Dental College, Hospital and research centre, Bangalore, for his guidance and for providing the opportunity to carry out this study.*

I extend my sincere thanks to ***Dr. Pruthvish.S,*** *Professor and Head, Department of Preventive and Community Medicine, M.S.Ramaiah Medical College, Bangalore,* ***Dr. Lalitha K.S ,Dr. Shalini Pradeep, Dr.Arjunan Isaac*** *for their guidance and advice that has helped me in accomplishing this task.*

I extend my humble thanks to our Principal, ***Dr. K.S. Ganapathy*** *for providing the opportunity to carry out this study. I am grateful to* ***Dr.Suresh K.P,*** *Statistician, for his valuable assistance, guidance and his help in statistical analysis.*

I would also like to express my thankfulness to all hospital authorities, staff, who have dedicated part of their valuable time for my study. I would like to express my gratitude to all ***My Colleagues*** *for their help, support, and co-operation throughout this study.*

I shall be forever indebted to all my ***Family Members*** *who have been constant sources of inspiration and encouragement. I wish to regard my deep appreciation for their immeasurable support, innumerable sacrifices, unstinted help and prayers without which I would not have been what I am today.*

Above all I bow my head in gratitude to ***Almighty*** *for bestowing his blessings on me and helping me make this effort a reality.*

Dr.Sushma.Rudraswamy

Table of Contents

ABSTRACT

Background and objectives: Growing urbanization has led to several changes in the healthcare sector. While on one hand, access to healthcare services are being provided to the community thereby resulting in the better health for all, improper management of biomedical waste emanating from these healthcare establishments has also given rise to many environmental and health problems.. Most hospitals are not actively involved in addressing this problem. Also, the staffs are not trained in the proper waste management procedures. The present interventional study was conducted to assess the knowledge, attitude and practice about hospital waste management, to provide training programme on hospital waste management and to assess the effect of training among the staff of dental teaching hospitals in Bangalore city.

Methodology: A specially prepared and pre-tested structured questionnaire was given to assess the knowledge, attitude and practices among the staff of dental teaching hospitals and collected personally. One day training programme on the hospital waste management was organized at each dental college. Intervention was evaluated by assessing improvements in their knowledge, change in attitude and practice scores after intervention in comparison to the base line scores.

Results: Two months after intervention there was a 24.4% improvement in knowledge among the dentists, 18.7% improvement among auxiliaries and 23.3% improvement ($p<0.001$, significant) among the attenders when compared to the baseline knowledge. There was 36.2% change in attitude among the dentists, 33.3% change among auxiliaries, 56.42% and among the attenders ($p<0.001$, significant) when compared to the baseline attitude. There was a 17.6% change in practice among the dentists, 16.4 % change among auxiliaries, and 4.4 % among the attenders when compared to the baseline practice.

Conclusion: The findings of this study suggest that a training programme increases the knowledge as well as the sense of responsibility resulting in change in attitude and practices. However, to implement an effective and sustainable hospital waste management system: budget support, allocation of resources and technical guidance is required. Large volumes of workload bureaucratic culture and slow percolation of decisions delays the changes that are mandated.

Keywords: Biomedical waste, Hospital waste management, Knowledge, Attitude, Practice.

INTRODUCTION

"Nothing on earth is more international than disease"
Paul Russel

Health and disease have no political or geographical boundaries. In the early Greek, Roman, Egyptian civilizations, the temple of god was used as hospitals. So, hospital is a place of almighty, a place to serve the patient. These are complex institutions which were frequented by people from every walk of life in the society without any distinction between age, sex, race and religion[1].

Growing urbanization has led to several changes in the healthcare sector. While on one hand, access to healthcare services are being provided to the community thereby resulting in the better health for all, improper management of hospital waste emanating from these healthcare establishments has also given rise to many environmental and health problems, thereby negating the benefits of the expanding health sector.

It is reported that for the first time the hospital waste management issue was discussed at a meeting convened by the World Health Organization regional office for Europe at Bergen, Norway in 1983. The seriousness of the issue was brought to limelight during the "beach wash- ups" of summer 1988. Investigation carried out by the Environment Protection Agency (EPA) of USA in this regard culminated in the passing of Medical Waste Tracking Act (MWTA), November 1988[2]. With the passage of time the problem has evolved as a global humanitarian issue.

Until fairly recently, hospital waste management was not generally considered an issue. In 1980s and 1990s concerns about exposure to human immunodeficiency virus (HIV) and hepatitis B virus (HBV) led to questions about potential risks inherent in hospital waste[3]. Thus hospital waste generation has become a prime concern due to its multidimensional ramifications as a risk factor to the health of patients, hospital staff and extending beyond the boundaries of the hospital establishment to the general populations. The management of hospital waste is still in its infancy all over the world. Now hospital waste management is one of the trust areas which are drawing the attention of health authorities and the Government. There is a lot of confusion and problems among the generators, operators, decision-makers and the general community about the safe management.

Hospital waste management has been brought into focus in India recently, particularly with the notification of the biomedical waste management and handling rules. The ministry of environment and forests, government of India notified the bio-medical waste (management and handling) rules on 27 th July 1998[4] .These rules have been formed in exercise of the powers conferred by sections 6, 8 and 25 of environmental protection act 1986. The rule makes it mandatory for the health care establishment to segregate, disinfect and dispose their waste in eco friendly manner. Clearly, statutory safeguards for biomedical waste management practice in Indian hospitals have still not achieved the desired standards.

Since last few years there has been rapid mushrooming of dental health care set ups catering the needs of people and thereby there is definite increase in the quantity of waste generated. According to a WHO report, around 85% of the hospital wastes are actually non hazardous, 10% are infective (hence, hazardous), and the remaining 5% are non-infectious but hazardous (chemical, pharmaceutical and radioactive). Dental Hospitals generates waste similar to other health care set ups which includes a large component of general waste and a smaller proportion of hazardous waste.

Biomedical waste generated in dental hospitals include sharps, body tissues, chemicals –fixers , mercury, silver thiosulfate, lead foils, fresh mix of amalgam, scrap amalgam etc. and used dental materials. To ensure compliance with the law, these materials must be properly handled, recycled, treated and/or disposed. But more often, in dental hospitals the general wastes and biomedical wastes are allowed to mix thereby rendering the general waste also toxic and hazardous. Most dental hospitals are not actively involved in addressing this problem.

In spite of the fact that the biomedical waste is a great health hazard, the awareness and knowledge regarding biomedical waste handling and disposal is abysmally low and scientific literature search show significant gap in the knowledge, attitude and practice among the staff about hospital waste management [6]. Also, the staffs are not trained in the proper waste management procedure which is the need of the hour. Recognizing this need we have to address these issues and provide training programme to impart training, knowledge dissemination, and provide an excellent platform for mooting innovative strategies to integrate "hospital waste management" as a corporate social responsibility, instead of mere social cost.

So, in this view, this study was the first of its kind to assess the knowledge, attitude and practice about hospital waste management and to impart training in proper hospital waste management procedure and to assess the effect of training among the staff of dental teaching hospitals in Bangalore city.

Let the wastes of "the sick" not contaminate the lives of "the healthy".

Aim

To study the knowledge, attitude and practice about hospital waste management and to assess the effect of training among the staff of dental teaching hospitals in Bangalore city.

Objectives

1. To study the knowledge, attitude and practices towards hospital waste management among staff of dental teaching colleges in Bangalore city.
2. To provide training programme on hospital waste management for the staff of dental teaching colleges in Bangalore city.
3. To assess the effectiveness of hospital waste management training programme on knowledge, attitude and practices among staff of dental teaching hospitals in Bangalore city.

REVIEW OF LITERATURE

Literature search show very limited scientific literature on the knowledge, attitude and practice about hospital waste management among staff of dental teaching hospitals, and also there are no studies done to assess the effectiveness of the training programme on hospital waste management among the staff of dental teaching hospitals. Hence only the related knowledge, attitude and practice studies are considered here.

A national survey[7] was conducted to investigate current procedures in New Zealand dental practices for disposal of clinical waste. A questionnaire was sent out to all dental practices in New Zealand. From three mailings 767 useable questionnaires were returned (71.3%) of those sent out, 79.0%, of those potentially valid. Responses indicated that 56.4% of dental practices disposed of bloody swabs into the waste paper bin, and 24.4% disposed of contaminated sharp items into the general household refuse collection. Qualitative interviews with dental practitioners revealed a lack of concern about disposal of contaminated waste into the general waste. The existence of legislation governing waste disposal was not sufficient to motivate many practitioners to comply with guidelines. In some areas there was no specialized waste disposal service available, but some dentists had rejected a specialized service on the grounds of cost or inconvenience.

A study[8] investigated the disposal of clinical waste within dental surgeries in Bangkok, Thailand. A questionnaire was sent to all dental practices in the Bangkok Metropolitan Area. The response rate was 57.7 per cent. Few dentists complied with all recommendations for the disposal of waste. Most waste was disposed of into the domestic rubbish stream.

A survey[9] was undertaken among 64 dentists working in a teaching hospital of New Delhi. A pre-tested self-administered questionnaire was used to assess knowledge and practices of biomedical waste management and infection control among these dentists. Questionnaire comprised question on disposal of infectious waste, legislation of biomedical waste management, usage of personal protective equipment and measures adopted to limit the spread of infection. The results showed that not all dentists were aware of the risks they were exposed to and only half of them observed infection control practices. In addition to this, majority of them were not aware of proper hospital waste management.

An investigation [10] at 37 randomly selected clinics in Ramallah and AI-Bireh cities: 31 private practices and 6 public/NGO clinics was done to know about disposal of dental waste. Dentists were interviewed regarding their disposal of different forms of dental waste. Disinfectants and X-ray processing solution were thrown down the drain. For sharps, 13.5% of dentists used puncture-resistant containers (only in the public/ NGO clinics), 45.9% discarded needles directly in the garbage after being recapped and 40.5% placed the used needles and blades in closed plastic bottles before throwing in the general garbage. Blood-soaked dressings and amalgam waste were also thrown in the garbage. While 10.75% of dentists were vaccinated against hepatitis B, 47% of the staff at private clinics were not.

A cross-sectional study[11] of 432 private dental practitioners in Bangalore City using a self-administered questionnaire was done to assess the knowledge, attitude and behavior of private dental practitioners on health care waste management in Bangalore City. 64.3% do not segregate waste before disposal and 47.6% hand over health care waste to street garbage collectors; 42.1% felt that there was a lack of waste management agency services and 16.9% felt that a lack of knowledge were the main hurdles. Dentists need education regarding health care waste disposal methods to improve their knowledge. A large proportion of the dentists are not practicing proper methods of health care waste disposal. The existence of legislation governing healthcare waste disposal is not sufficient alone to motivate many practitioners to comply with guidelines.

There is limited relevant scientific literature available with respect to knowledge, attitude and practice about hospital waste management among the staff of dental teaching hospitals, and since dental settings are a part of health care set ups the related studies on health care set ups are considered for review.

A research[12] project was conducted to compare waste management in five different European hospitals. The project examined disposal practices, applicable regulations, available infrastructure, and the organization of waste collection and disposal in the hospitals. Regulation and guidance documents relevant to waste management were collected and compared and analysis of waste was undertaken to obtain more detailed information about waste composition and waste segregation. Workshops were held to compare disposal practice in the different hospitals, the influence of legal stipulation and available local infrastructure. The study included basic consideration such as the health and safety of patients and personnel, handling, level of staff knowledge and available infrastructure.

A Survey[13] was conducted in Pondicherry, Karaikal, Mahe and Yanam to determine the awareness about waste management policy and practices. Attitude related to the issue was also ascertained. Data was collected from all sections of employees in health care settings. To document the practices, photographs were also taken. Overall response rate was 82%. More than half (52%) of the respondents were not aware of the existence of a legislation and majority (72%) not aware of authorization. Vast majority (74%) did not use any color coding and only a very small percentage (15%) used the bio-hazard symbol. Maintaining a register and auditing virtually did not exist. Majority (80%) regarded this as an issue that needs to be tackled.

A study[14] was conducted to know the management of bio-medical waste: awareness and practices in a district of Gujarat. With the objective of assessing the level of awareness about the various aspects of biomedical waste and disposal practices by the medical practitioners this study was conducted. It was a cross sectional study done in 30 hospitals which were randomly selected from Sabarkantha district, Gujarat. The doctors and auxiliary staff of those 30 hospitals were the study population. While all the doctors knew about the existence of the law related to biomedical waste but details were not known. Doctors were aware of risk of HIV and Hepatitis B and C, whereas auxiliary staff had very poor knowledge about it. There was no effective waste segregation, collection, transportation and disposal system at any hospital in the district. There is an immediate and urgent need to train and educate all doctors and the staff to adopt an effective waste management practice.

A study[15] on Knowledge, Attitude and Practice (KAP) was carried out in a tertiary level teaching hospital. The KAP study enrolled 156 respondents, representing doctors and nurses from selected patient care areas. Here, a significant gap was observed in the knowledge, attitude and practice of the consultants, residents and scientists with regard to biomedical waste disposal, to their Knowledge/understanding on the subject. Nursing professionals on the other hand, had an edge over the clinicians as far as attitude and practice of biomedical waste management is concerned although their knowledge on the subject was relatively low. The paramedical staff including laboratory and housekeeping staff had least understanding on the subject, but had higher positive attitude with more practical habits, which may be attributed to strict instructions by authorities and fear for any punitive action.

A cross-sectional survey[16] was conducted in eight teaching hospitals of Karachi to evaluate the current practices of segregation approaches, storage arrangements, and collection and disposal systems. The instrument of research was a self administered questionnaire, with four sections, relating to the general information of the institution, administrative information,

information regarding Health Waste Management personnel and a check-list of Hospital Waste Management activities. Out of eight hospitals visited 2 (25%) were segregating sharps, pathological waste, chemical, infectious, pharmaceutical and pressurized containers at source. For handling potentially dangerous waste, two (25%) hospitals provided essential protective gears to its waste handlers. Only one (12.5%) hospital arranged training sessions for its waste handling staff regularly. Five (62.5%) hospitals had storage areas but mostly it was not protected from access of scavengers. No record of waste was generally maintained. Only two (25%) hospitals had well documented guidelines for waste management and a proper waste management team.

A cross sectional study[17] was conducted in Hamidia hospital to assess the knowledge of the personnel (working staff including doctors, nurses, ward boys, and sweepers). Although the level of knowledge was more among doctors and nurses as compared to ward boys and sweepers. Almost all the respondents among doctors and nurses were aware that improper management of waste causes health hazards while 40-60% of ward boys and sweepers were aware about this fact. All respondents felt that closed containers should be used for collecting waste.

A survey[18] was conducted to study the existing medical waste management (MWM) systems in Tanzanian hospitals during a nationwide health-care waste management-training programme conducted from 2003 to 2005. The aim of the programme was to enable health workers to establish MWM systems in their health facilities aimed at improving infection prevention and control and occupational health aspects. During the training sessions, a questionnaire was prepared and circulated to collect information on the MWM practices existing in hospitals in eight regions of the Tanzania. The analysis showed that increased population and poor MWM systems as well as expanded use of disposables were the main reasons for increased medical wastes in hospitals. Some hospitals were using untrained casual laborers in medical waste management and general cleanliness. The knowledge level in MWM issues was low among the health workers. It is concluded that hospital waste management in Tanzania was poor. There was need for proper training and management regarding awareness and practices of medical waste management to cover all carders of health workers.

The study[19] pertains to the biomedical waste management practices at Balrampur Hospital. The study shows that infectious and non-infectious wastes are dumped together within the hospital premises, resulting in a mixing of the two, which are then disposed of with municipal waste at the dumping sites in the city. All types of wastes are collected in common bins placed outside the patients wards. The results of the study demonstrate the need for strict enforcement of legal provisions and a better environmental management system for the disposal of biomedical waste in the Balrampur Hospital, as well as other healthcare establishments in Lucknow.

A study[20] was conducted to know the overview of biomedical waste management in selected Governorates in Egypt. Five hospitals and ten primary healthcare settings were surveyed using a modified survey questionnaire for waste management. This questionnaire was obtained from the World Health Organization (WHO), with the aim of assessing the processing systems for biomedical waste disposal. Researchers found that biomedical waste is inadequately processed in hospitals and primary healthcare settings due to the absence of written policies and protocols. Accordingly, healthcare staff, patients, the community and the environment may be negatively affected by exposure to the hazards of biomedical waste. The development of waste management policies, plans, and protocols are strongly recommended, in addition to establishing training programs on proper waste management for all healthcare workers.

A study[21] done with the aim to assess the awareness about biomedical waste and its disposal practices at the SMHS Hospital of Kashmir, this study included 150 subjects including medical and paramedical staff. The awareness was significantly satisfactory among doctors and nurses whereas there is lack of knowledge and awareness among laboratory personnel and other members of the paramedical staff, which needs effective teaching and training to prevent adverse outcome on human health.

A study[22] was conducted in Andhra Pradesh, Maharashtra and Uttar Pradesh in India. Hospitals/nursing homes and private medical practitioners in urban as well as rural areas and those from the private as well as the government sector were covered. Information on (a) awareness of bio-medical waste management rules, (b) training undertaken and (c) practices with respect to segregation, use of colour coding, sharps management, access to common waste management facilities and disposal was collected. Awareness of Bio-medical Waste Management Rules was better among hospital staff in comparison with private medical practitioners and awareness was marginally higher among those in urban areas in comparison with those in rural areas. Training gained momentum only after the dead-line for compliance was over. Segregation and use of colour codes revealed gaps, which need correction. About 70% of the healthcare facilities used a needle cutter/destroyer for sharps management. Access to Common Waste Management facilities was low at about 35%. Dumping biomedical waste on the roads outside the hospital is still prevalent and access to Common waste facilities is still limited. Surveillance, monitoring and penal machinery was found to be deficient and these require strengthening to improve compliance with the Bio-medical Waste Management Rules and to safeguard the health of employees, patients and communities.

This study[23] investigated the medical waste management practices used by hospitals in northern Jordan. A comprehensive inspection survey was conducted for all 21 hospitals located in the study area. Field visits were conducted to provide information on the different medical waste management aspects. The results reported focused on the level of medical waste segregation, treatment and disposal options. The results also showed that segregation of various medical waste types in the hospitals has not been conducted properly. The study revealed the need for training and capacity building programs of all employees involved in the medical waste management.

MATERIALS AND METHODS

This study was conducted to assess the knowledge, attitude and practices towards hospital waste management among staff of dental teaching colleges in Bangalore city. To provide training programme on hospital waste management for the staff of dental teaching colleges in Bangalore city, and to assess the effectiveness of hospital waste management training programme on knowledge, attitude and practices among staff of dental teaching hospitals in Bangalore city.

OBTAINING APPROVAL FROM THE AUTHORITIES

ETHICAL COMMITTEE CLEARANCE

The ethical clearance was obtained from the ethical committee of The Oxford Dental College, Hospital and Research Centre prior to the start of the study

REQUIRED INFORMATION ABOUT THE STUDY AREAS

All the required and relevant information regarding dental colleges that were approved/ recognized by DCI was obtained from the website of the Dental Council of India. In the Bangalore City there are 16 dental colleges approved/ recognized by DCI serving the oral health care needs of the population at large.

SAMPLE SIZE:

Total number of the dental teaching hospitals approved by DCI present in Bangalore city was sixteen. For the purpose of conducting this study cluster sampling procedure was adopted. Fifty percent of the total sixteen dental teaching hospitals that is eight is selected using random selection considering the constraints of limited resources like manpower, finance, and administrative logistics. These eight colleges constituted the cluster for conducting the study. A total population comprising of 283 Dentist, 32 Auxillary, and 76 Attenders were available from these eight dental teaching hospitals in Bangalore city.

Inclusion criteria:

- Staff of dental teaching hospitals willing to participate (dentists, dental auxiliary, attender)

Exclusion criteria:

- Staff of dental teaching hospitals not willing to participate
- Office staff, drivers, staff directly or indirectly not involved in hospital waste generation.

PILOT STUDY

A pilot study was performed on the study population prior to the start of the study in one of the dental teaching hospitals in the month of November 2008. Expert opinion regarding the questionnaire was sought. The pilot study served as a preliminary study to identify any organizational problems, and to check the validity of questionnaire. To check the internal consistency of the questionnaire, the questionnaire was distributed to the dentists and dental auxiliaries and collected back by the investigator on two different days. The results thus obtained were subjected to statistical analysis. Cronbachs alpha value of 0.82 showed good internal consistency of the questionnaire. Similarly the questionnaire for attenders was also checked for internal consistency, which showed good internal consistency with Cronbachs alpha value of 0.84.

Results from this pilot study highlighted the need for minor revisions in the questionnaire. In the pilot study, some questions were unclear to participants; these were revised. The results of the pilot study were discussed with the Professor (Guide). Modifications were made wherever necessary and final study was planned and carried out.

SCHEDULE OF THE STUDY

The project was systematically scheduled to spread over a period of 6 months from April 2009 to September 2009. A detailed weekly and monthly schedule was prepared well in advance by informing and obtaining consent from authorities of respective dental teaching hospital. Even though a detailed schedule plan was prepared well in advance, few adjustments and changes had to be made while working it out practically.

IMPLEMENTING THE STUDY

BASE LINE DATA

Administrator was given a questionnaire to collect the information about hospital waste management, existing policy and practices in their respective dental teaching hospitals.

A specially prepared, and pre-tested structured questionnaire, was given to assess the knowledge, attitude and practices among the staff of dental teaching hospitals and collected personally.

For Dentist and Dental Auxilliary the questionnaire was in English consisting of a set of 30 questions which was further categorized in three sets with 10 questions each on knowledge, attitude and practice. And for Attenders the questionnaire was in Kannada consisting of a set of 15 questions which was further categorized in three sets with 5 questions each on knowledge, attitude and practice.

Questionnaire took less than 15 min to answer. All the answers were kept confidential and were not depicted against their identity.

In each institution the following elements were studied using checklist i.e segregation, colour coding, disinfection, containment, personal protective equipment, reporting of injuries, display of standard operating protocols, in house transport and disposal.

DETAILS OF THE INTERVENTION

One day training programme on the hospital waste management was organized at each dental college. Training was delivered by experts in the field of hospital waste management. Training was given in English to the Dentist and Dental Auxiliary and the local (Kannada) language for the Attenders. Learning media used was Audiovisual Aid- LCD projector.

The duration of training per each cadre was for one and half hour which was interactive, participatory and task focused. The focus of the training was on importance of need to manage the waste in hospitals, the various aspects of management like segregation, disinfection, colour coding……, getting them to appreciate that mismanagement of hospital waste puts if not the community to risk at least their lesser privileged colleagues in the hospital, and clearly identifying each ones roles and responsibilities.

The training programme for Dentist and Dental Auxiliary was in three sessions, first session was on "*Introduction to hospital waste management*", giving a brief insight about the sources, classification, health hazards and current scenario in regard to hospital waste management. The second session was on "*Options available and best practices*" for managing various dental wastes like mercury, lead foil, x-ray solution and others. The third session was on "*Tips for development of action plan*" which included biomedical waste management Rules, Steps for waste management, Health and safety principles of workers and post exposure prophylaxis.

The training programme for the Attenders was focused on need to manage the waste in hospitals, segregation and colour coding, personal protective equipment and post exposure prophylaxis.

The training module included slide presentations, manual on dental hospital waste management, and posters. The overall aim of training was to develop awareness of health, safety and environment issue relating to hospital waste and how these can affect employees in their daily work.

Though several attempts were made to involve each and every participant, still it was not possible to enroll all of them in the study. This was the limitation in the study. So, only the participants who attended training programme were given post intervention questionnaire and were considered for statistical analysis.

POST INTERVENTION DATA

Two months after initial training, the same baseline questionnaire was administered to the staff i.e. Dentist, Dental Auxillary and Attenders and monitoring of the waste management practices was documented using the same check list, used earlier.

EVALUATION OF THE INTERVENTION

Intervention was evaluated by assessing improvements in their knowledge, change in the attitude and practice scores after intervention in comparison to the base line scores. This comparison involved mean and percentage changes in their knowledge, attitude and practice on the hospital waste management. The questionnaire given For Dentist and Dental Auxilliary consisted of a set of 30 questions.

The questionnaire contained 10 questions regarding knowledge on hospital waste management. The correct answers were given a score of 1 and the wrong answers were given a score of 0. So, the knowledge score for an individual could range from a minimum of 0 to a maximum of 10. Also, there were 10 questions regarding attitude. The option strongly disagree were given a score of 1, disagree 2, don't know 3, agree 4, strongly agree 5. So, the attitude score for an individual could range from a minimum of 1 to a maximum of 50. And for the negative questions, the scoring was done appropriately giving highest score for the right attitude. There were 10 questions regarding practice. One of the questions had 4 subsets of questions. The correct answers were given a score of 1 and the wrong answers were given a score of 0. So, the practice score for an individual could range from a minimum of 1 to a maximum of 13.

And for Attenders the questionnaire consisted of a set of 15 questions. The questionnaire contained 5 questions regarding knowledge on hospital waste management. And one of the questions had 3 subsets of questions. The correct answers were given a score of 1 and the wrong answers were given a score of 0. So, the knowledge score for an individual could range from a minimum of 0 to a maximum of 7. Also, there were 5 questions regarding attitude. The correct answers were given a score of 1 and the wrong answers were given a score of 0. So, the attitude score for an individual could range from a minimum of 0 to a maximum of 5. And there were 5 questions regarding practice. And one of the questions had 3 subsets of questions. The correct answers were given a score of 1 and the wrong answers were given a score of 0. So, the practice score for an individual could range from a minimum of 0 to a maximum of 7.

Evaluation was also done using the check list to document the existing practices.

STATISTICAL ANALYSIS [24, 25, 26]

Descriptive statistical analysis has been carried out in the present study. The data so obtained from the study sample was compiled; systematized, tabulated and master table was prepared. SPSS version 15.0 (SPSS Pty Ltd, Chicago, IL, USA) was used for the statistical analyses. From the master table the required data were picked up for data presentation as tables. The data was subjected to statistical analysis wherever required using inferential statistical techniques

Results on continuous measurements are presented on Mean ± SD (Min-Max) and results on categorical measurements are presented in Number (%). Significance is assessed at 5 % level of significance. Student t test (two tailed, dependent) has been used to find the significance of study parameters on continuous scale with in each group. Paired proportion test has been used to find the significance of proportion before and after intervention. Cohen's d Effect size is calculated to measure the strength of the relationship between two variables.

1. Cronbach's Alpha: measure of the internal consistency reliability

$$\alpha = \frac{N \cdot \bar{c}}{(\bar{v} + (N-1) \cdot \bar{c})}$$

Where N = number of items

$\bar{c}$ = average inter-item covariance among the items

$\bar{v}$ = the average variance.

2. Student t-test for paired comparisons

Objective: To investigate the significance of the difference between single population means. No assumption is made about the population variances

$$t = \frac{(\bar{x}1 - \bar{x}2)}{s / \sqrt{n}}$$

where $s = \sqrt{\sum (di - \bar{d})^2 / n - 1}$ and di is the difference formed for each pair of observations

3. Significant figures

+ Suggestive significance (P value: 0.05<P<0.10)

* Moderately significant (P value:0.01<P ≤ 0.05)

** Strongly significant (P value : P≤0.01)

4. Cohen's d Effect size:

$$d = \frac{\bar{x}_1 - \bar{x}_2}{s}$$

Where

$\bar{x}_1 - \bar{x}_2$ is the difference between means

's' is the pooled standard deviation and is calculated by the formula

$$s = \sqrt{\frac{(n_1 - 1)s_1^2 + (n_2 - 1)s_2^2}{n_1 + n_2}}$$

Less than 0.20 – No effect.

0.20– 0.50 – Small (S) effect

0.50 – 0.80 – Medium (M) effect

0.80 – 1.2 – Large (L) effect

More than 1.2 – Very large (VL) effect

Statistical software: The Statistical software namely SPSS 15.0, and Systat 11.0 were used for the analysis of the data and Microsoft word and Excel have been used to generate graphs, tables etc.

RESULTS

An interventional study was conducted to assess the effectiveness of hospital waste management training programme on knowledge, attitude and practices among staff of dental teaching hospitals in Bangalore city. Study participants comprised of 259 Dentists, 26 auxiliaries and 69 attenders from eight dental teaching hospitals in Bangalore city.

Age and gender distribution of study participants (At base line)

Table 1: Age and Gender Distribution among Dentists

Dentist	Male		Female		Total	
	No	%	No	%	No	%
20-29	32	25.4	47	35.3	79	30.5
30-39	72	57.1	70	52.6	142	54.8
40-49	13	10.3	14	10.5	27	10.4
50-59	9	7.1	2	1.5	11	4.2
Total	126	100.0	133	100.0	259	100.0
Mean ± SD	34.25±7.21		32.75±6.25		33.48±6.76	

Table 1 shows the age and gender distribution of the dentist participated in the study. Among the 126 male dentists, 25.4 %(n-32) were in the age group of 20-29 years, 57.1% (n-72) in 30-39 years, 10.3 %(n-13) in 40-49 years, 7.1 %(n-9) in 50-59 years respectively. The mean age of male dentist was 34.25±7.21. Among the133 female dentists, 35.3 %(n-47) were in the age group of 20-29 years, 52.6.1% (n-70) in 30-39 years, 10.5 %(n-14) in 40-49 years, 1.5 % (n-2) in 50-59 years respectively. The mean age of female dentist was 32.75±6.25. Among 259 total dentists, 30.5 %(n-79) were in the age group of 20-29 years, 54.8% (n-142) in 30-39 years, 10.4 %(n-27) in 40-49 years, 4.2 %(n-11) in 50-59 years respectively with the mean age of 33.48±6.76.

Table 2: Age and Gender Distribution among Auxiliaries

Auxiliary staff	Male		Female		Total	
	No	%	No	%	No	%
20-29	3	20.0	6	54.5	9	34.6
30-39	7	46.7	3	27.3	10	38.5
40-49	3	20.0	1	9.1	4	15.4
50-59	2	13.3	1	9.1	3	11.5
Total	15	100.0	11	100.0	26	100.0
Mean ± SD	36.33±8.12		33.09±8.63		34.96±8.33	

Table 2 shows the age and gender distribution of the Auxiliaries participated in the study. Among 15 male Auxiliaries, 20.0 %(n-3) were in the age group of 20-29 years, 46.7% (n-7) in 30-39 years, 20 %(n-3) in 40-49 years, 13.3%(n-2) in 50-59 years respectively. The mean age of male Auxiliaries was 36.33±8.12. Among the 11 female Auxiliaries, 54.5 %(n-6) were in the age group of 20-29 years, 27.3% (n-3) in 30-39 years, 9.1 %(n-1) in 40-49 years, 9.1 %(n-1) in 50-59 years respectively. The mean age of female Auxiliaries, was 33.09±8.63. Among 26 total Auxiliaries, 34.6 %(n-9) were in the age group of 20-29 years, 38.5% (n-10) in 30-39 years, 15.4 %(n-4) in 40-49 years, 11.5 %(n-3) in 50-59 years respectively with the mean age of 34.96±8.33.

Table 3: Age and Gender Distribution among attenders

Age in years	Male		Female		Total	
	No	%	No	%	No	%
20-29	6	19.4	3	7.9	9	13.0
30-39	7	22.6	18	47.4	25	36.2
40-49	16	51.6	17	44.7	33	47.8
50-59	2	6.5	0	0.0	2	2.9

Total	31	100.0	38	100.0	69	100.0
Mean ± SD	37.35±6.99		36.89±6.72		37.08±6.79	

Table 3 shows the age and gender distribution of the Attenders participated in the study. Among the 31 male Attenders, 19.4%(n-6) were in the age group of 20-29 years, 22.6% (n-7) in 30-39 years, 51.6 %(n-16) in 40-49 years, 6.5%(n-2) in 50-59 years respectively. The mean age of male Attenders, was 37.35±6.99. Among the 38 female Attenders 7.9 %(n-3) were in the age group of 20-29 years, 47.4% (n-18) in 30-39 years, 44.7 %(n-17) in 40-49 years respectively. The mean age of female Attenders was 36.89±6.72. Among a total of 69 Attenders, 13.0% (n-9) were in the age group of 20-29 years, 36.2% (n-25) in 30-39 years, 47.8 %(n-33) in 40-49 years, 2.9%(n-2) in 50-59 years respectively with mean age of 37.08±6.79.

AT BASELINE

Table 4: Assessment of knowledge among dentists regarding hospital waste management

Knowledge Questions	Total dentists(n= 259)	
	No	%
Q1. Segregation of waste into different categories should be done at	148	57.1
Q2. Disinfection before disposal helps to	213	82.2
Q3. Identify the biohazard symbol	175	67.6
Q 4. Which of the following is not an acceptable technique for the handling of sharp needles?	21	8.1
Q5. The presence of personal protective equipments	236	91.1
Q6. The main risk posed by needle stick injury is exposure of the workers to blood- borne viruses	202	78.0
Q7. Infectious waste is given the colour code of	179	69.1
Q8. Hepatitis-B immunization for health care workers	245	94.6
Q9. After possible HIV exposure in health care worker	243	93.8
Q10. Mercury and excess amalgam should be	232	89.6

A total of 259 dentists answered the questionnaire at baseline. With regards to the first question, 57.1% of them answered correctly that Segregation of waste into different categories should be done at the point of generation. 82.2% answered correctly that the purpose of "Disinfection before disposal" reduce the risk of transmission of infection, strengthen and support the overall standards of hospital hygiene and also prevents the spread of multidrug-resistant and other nosocomial pathogen. A total of 67.6% of dentist identified the biohazard symbol correctly. With respect to the question regarding technique which is not acceptable for the handling of sharp needles, 82.6% answered correctly that disposing needle in general trash bag was not acceptable. Question 5 assessed the participants' knowledge regarding personal protective equipments for which 91.1% answered correctly that personal protective equipments prevents the transmission of infection from patient to dental health care personnel and from dental health care personnel to patient . A total of 78% knew that there could be risk posed to the workers by exposure of blood- borne viruses like Hepatitis-B (HBV), Hepatitis-C (HCV) Human immunodeficiency virus (HIV) with needle stick injury. When asked to identify the colour code for Infectious waste, yellow colour was correctly identified by 67.1% of dentists. 94.6 % of the dentists said that Hepatitis-B immunization for health care workers was compulsory and 93.8% responded correctly that post exposure prophylaxis should be initiated as soon as possible after possible HIV exposure in health care worker. 89.6 % knew that mercury and excess amalgam should be stored in water/ fixer solution.

Table 5: Assessment of attitude among dentists regarding hospital waste management

Attitude Questions	Total dentists (n= 259)	
	No	%
Q11. Segregation of waste at source increases the risk of injury to waste handlers	92	35.5
Q12. Decontamination / disinfection reduces chances of infection	139	53.7
Q13. Infectious waste should be put in yellow colored plastic bag with bio hazard symbol	130	50.2
Q14. Containment of sharps does not help in safe management of hospital waste	71	27.4
Q15. Occupational safety of waste handlers is a must	181	69.9
Q16. Reporting of needle stick injury is an extra burden on work.	93	35.9
Q17. Use of colour code for segregation of waste is a must	180	69.5
Q18. Hepatitis-B immunization prevents transmission of hospital acquired infection	90	34.7
Q19. Post exposure prophylaxis should be initiated as soon as possible	185	71.4
Q20. Excess mercury/ amalgam should be stored in water or fixer solution	157	60.6

33.5% strongly of dentists disagreed that segregation of waste at source increases the risk of injury to waste handlers. 53.7% of them strongly agreed decontamination / disinfection reduces chances of infection at baseline. 50.2% strongly agreed that Infectious waste should be put in yellow colored plastic bag. 27.4% strongly disagreed to the statement "Containment of sharps does not help in safe management of hospital waste". A total of 69.9% of dentists strongly agreed that occupational safety of waste handlers is a must. 35.9% strongly disagreed that reporting of needle stick injury is an extra burden on work. 69.5% strongly agreed that the use of colour codes for segregation of waste is a must. 34.7% strongly agreed that Hepatitis-B immunization prevents transmission of hospital acquired infection and 71.4% strongly agreed to the statement "Post exposure prophylaxis should be initiated as soon as possible". A total of 60.6% of dentists strongly agreed that excess mercury/ amalgam should be stored in water or fixer solution.

Table 6: Assessment of practice among dentists regarding hospital waste management

Practice Question	Total dentists(n= 259)	
	No	%
Q21. Do you segregate waste into different categories at the point of origin?	215	83.0
Q22. Do you treat sharp waste prior to disposal?	204	78.8
Q23. Do you dispose infectious waste in yellow colored plastic bag having biohazard symbol	215	83.0
Q24. Do you use heavy duty (puncture proof) plastic container to collect the waste sharps ?	192	74.1
Q25. Do you use personal protective devices		
Apron	254	98.1
Mask	256	98.8
Gloves	256	98.8
Goggles	175	67.6
Q26. Do you follow system of recording and reporting of injuries/accidents?	160	61.8
Q27. Do you follow colour code for segregation of waste?	215	83.0

A total of 83% of dentists said that they segregate waste into different categories at the point of origin. 78.8% responded yes for treating sharp waste prior to disposal. 83% disposed infectious waste in yellow colored plastic bag having biohazard symbol. 74.1% use heavy duty (puncture proof) plastic container to collect the waste sharps.

98.1% of dentists used apron, 98.8% used mouth mask and gloves, 67.6% used goggles as personal protective devices and. 61.8% followed system of recording and reporting of injuries/accidents. A total of 83% of dentists followed colour code for segregation of waste at baseline. 96.5% had taken vaccination against Hepatitis B and 85.7% followed Post exposure prophylaxis following percutaneous exposure. 82.2% of them stored excess mercury/amalgam in water or fixer solution.

Table 7: Assessment of knowledge among auxiliaries regarding hospital waste management

Knowledge Questions	**Total Auxiliaries (n= 26)**	
	No	**%**
Q1. Segregation of waste into different categories should be done at	20	76.9
Q2. Disinfection before disposal helps to	22	84.6
Q3. Identify the biohazard symbol	18	69.2
Q 4. Which of the following is not an acceptable technique for the handling of sharp needles?	24	92.3
Q5. The presence of personal protective equipments	24	92.3
Q6. The main risk posed by needle stick injury is exposure of the workers to blood- borne viruses	22	84.6
Q7. Infectious waste is given the colour code of	17	65.4
Q8. Hepatitis-B immunization for health care workers	23	88.5
Q9. After possible HIV exposure in health care worker	26	100.0
Q10. Mercury and excess amalgam should be	13	50.0

A total of 26 auxiliaries answered the questionnaire at baseline. With regards to the first question, 76.9% auxiliaries answered correctly that Segregation of waste into different categories should be done at the point of generation answered correctly. 84.6% answered correctly that the purpose of "Disinfection before disposal" reduce the risk of transmission of infection, strengthen and support the overall standards of hospital hygiene and also prevents the spread of multidrug- resistant and other nosocomial pathogens. A total of 69.2% of auxiliaries identified the biohazard symbol correctly. With respect to the question regarding technique which is not acceptable for the handling of sharp needles, 92.3% of them answered correctly that disposing needle in general trash bag was not acceptable. Question 5 assessed the participants' knowledge regarding personal protective equipments for which 92.3% answered correctly that personal protective equipments prevents the transmission of infection from patient to dental health care personnel and from dental health care personnel to patient. A total of 84.6% of auxiliaries knew that there could be risk posed to the workers by exposure of blood- borne viruses like Hepatitis-B (HBV), Hepatitis-C (HCV) Human immunodeficiency virus (HIV) with needle stick injury. When asked to identify the colour code for Infectious waste yellow colour was correctly identified by 65.4% of auxiliaries. 88.5 % of the auxiliaries said that Hepatitis-B immunization for health care workers was compulsory and 100% responded correctly that post exposure prophylaxis should be initiated as soon as possible after possible HIV exposure in health care worker. 50% of them knew that mercury and excess amalgam should be Stored in water/ fixer solution.

Table 8: Assessment of attitude among auxiliaries regarding hospital waste management

Attitude Questions	Total Auxiliaries (n= 26)	
	No	%
Q11. Segregation of waste at source increases the risk of injury to waste handlers	16	61.5
Q12. Decontamination / disinfection reduces chances of infection	14	53.8
Q13. Infectious waste should be put in yellow colored plastic bag with bio hazard symbol	15	57.7
Q14. Containment of sharps does not help in safe management of hospital waste	9	34.6
Q15. Occupational safety of waste handlers is a must	13	50.0
Q16. Reporting of needle stick injury is an extra burden on work.	9	34.6
Q17. Use of colour code for segregation of waste is a must	12	46.2
Q18. Hepatitis-B immunization prevents transmission of hospital acquired infection	17	65.4
Q19. Post exposure prophylaxis should be initiated as soon as possible	17	65.4
Q20. Excess mercury/ amalgam should be stored in water or fixer solution	20	76.9

61.5% of auxiliaries strongly disagreed that segregation of waste at source increases the risk of injury to waste handlers. 53.8% strongly agreed decontamination / disinfection reduces chances of infection at baseline. 57.7% strongly agreed that Infectious waste should be put in yellow colored plastic bag. 34.6% strongly disagreed to the statement "Containment of sharps does not help in safe management of hospital waste". A total of 50% of auxiliaries strongly agreed that occupational safety of waste handlers is a must. 34.6% strongly disagreed that reporting of needle stick injury is an extra burden on work. 46.2% strongly agreed use of colour code for segregation of waste is a must. 65.4% strongly agreed that Hepatitis-B immunization prevents transmission of hospital acquired infection and 65.4% strongly agreed to the statement "Post exposure prophylaxis should be initiated as soon as possible". A total of 76.9% of auxiliaries strongly agreed that excess mercury/ amalgam should be stored in water or fixer solution.

Table 9: Assessment of practice among auxiliaries regarding hospital waste management

Practice Question	**Total auxiliaries(n= 26)**	
	No	**%**
Q21. Do you segregate waste into different categories at the point of origin?	14	53.8
Q22. Do you treat sharp waste prior to disposal?	21	80.8
Q23. Do you dispose infectious waste in yellow colored plastic bag having biohazard symbol	19	73.1
Q24. Do you use heavy duty (puncture proof) plastic container to collect the waste sharps ?	23	88.5
Q25. Do you use personal protective devices Apron	20	76.9
Mask	25	96.2
Gloves	26	100.0
Goggles	19	73.1
Q26. Do you follow system of recording and reporting of injuries/accidents?	19	73.1
Q27. Do you follow colour code for segregation of waste?	18	69.2
Q28. Have you taken vaccination against hepatitis B?	23	88.5

Q29. Following percutaneous exposure do you follow Post exposure prophylaxis?	24	92.3
Q30. Do you store excess mercury/amalgam in water or fixer solution?	21	80.8

A total of 53.8% of auxiliaries said that they segregate waste into different categories at the point of origin. 80.8% responded yes for treating sharp waste prior to disposal. 73.1% disposed infectious waste in yellow colored plastic bag having biohazard symbol. 88.5% use heavy duty (puncture proof) plastic container to collect the waste sharps. 76.9% of auxiliaries used apron. 96.2% used mouth mask and 100% used gloves 73.1% used goggles as personal protective devices. 73.1% followed system of recording and reporting of injuries/accidents. A total of 69.2% of auxiliaries followed colour code for segregation of waste at baseline. 88.5% had taken vaccination against Hepatitis B and 92.3% followed Post exposure prophylaxis following percutaneous exposure. 80.8% of them stored excess mercury/amalgam in water or fixer solution.

Table 10: Assessment of knowledge among attenders regarding hospital waste management

Knowledge Questions	Total Attenders (n=69)	
	No	%
Q1. Identify the biohazard symbol	42	60.9
Q2. Infectious waste should be disposed of in which the colour code bag	49	71.0
Q3. Exposure to needle stick injury to workers may cause which disease	30	43.4
Q4. Should you use personal protective devices while handling hospital waste? Apron	63	91.3
Gloves	60	86.9
Mask	51	73.9
Q5. Disposing needle and waste sharps in general trash bag is a safe procedure	52	75.4

A total of 60.9% of participants identified the biohazard symbol. 71% knew infectious waste should be disposed of in yellow colour code bag. 46.4% of attenders correctly identified the disease caused by exposure to needle stick injury. Among the attenders 91.3%, 86.9%, and 73.9% knew apron, gloves; mouth mask should be used as a personal protective device while handling hospital waste respectively. 75.4% of them knew disposing needle and waste sharps in general trash bag is not a safe procedure.

Table 11: Assessment of attitudes among attenders regarding hospital waste management

Attitude Questions	Total Attenders(n=69)	
	No	%
Q6. Is it necessary to segregate waste into different categories at the point of origin?	57	82.6
Q7. Reporting of needle stick injury is an extra burden on work.	16	23.2
Q8. Segregation of waste at source increases the risk of injury to waste handlers	37	53.6
Q9. Is it necessary to take vaccination against hepatitis B?	38	55.1
Q10. Hepatitis-B immunization prevents transmission of hospital acquired infection	36	52.2

82.6% of attenders said that it is necessary to segregate waste into different categories at the point of origin. A total of 23.2% of them said reporting of needle stick injury is not an extra burden on work at baseline. 53.6 % agreed that Segregation of waste at source does not increase the risk of injury to waste handlers. 55.1% felt it is necessary to take vaccination against hepatitis B. 52.2% agreed that Hepatitis-B immunization prevents transmission of hospital acquired infection.

Table 12: Assessment of practices among attenders regarding hospital waste management

Practice Questions	Total Attenders (n-69)	
	No	%
Q11. Do you segregate waste into different categories at the point of origin?	61	88.4
Q12. Do you use personal protective devices? Apron	61	88.4
Gloves	63	91.3
Mask	53	76.8
Q13. Do you dispose infectious waste in yellow colored plastic	65	94.2
Q14. Do you follow system of recording and reporting of injuries/accidents?	23	33.3
Q15. Have you taken vaccination against hepatitis B?	18	26.1

A total of 88.4% of attenders said that they segregate waste into different categories at the point of origin. 88.4% 91.3% and 76.8% of the attenders used apron, gloves and mouth mask respectively. 94.2% of them disposed infectious waste in yellow colored plastic bag. 33.3% followed system of recording and reporting of injuries/accidents. 26.1% of them had taken vaccination against Hepatitis B.

Table 13, Graph 1: Drop out analysis

Study group	Dentists		Auxiliaries		Attenders	
	No	%	No	%	No	%
Pre intervention	259	100	26	100	69	100
Post intervention	177	68.3%	19	73%	54	78.2%
Total no of drop outs	82	31.6%	7	26.9%	15	21.7%

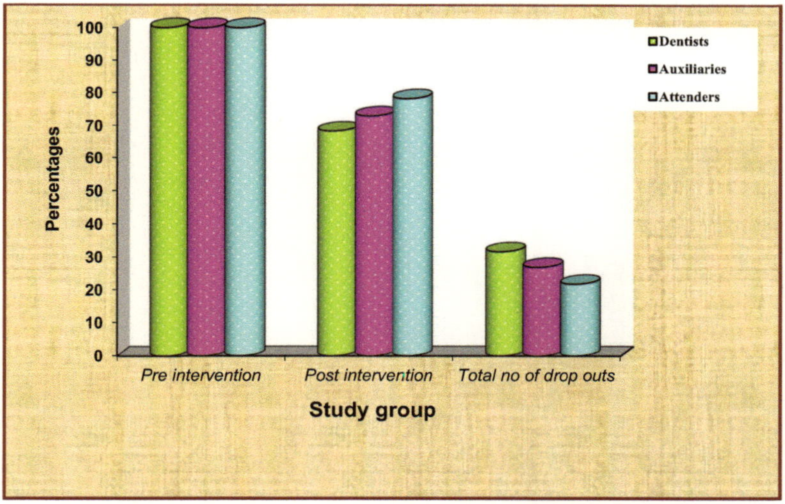

At baseline, a total of 259 dentists, 26 auxiliaries and 69 attenders formed the study group. Among them 177 dentists, 19 auxiliaries and 54 attenders attended the training programme and answered the post-intervention questionnaire. The dropout rate was 31.6% among dentists, 26.9% among auxiliaries and 21.7% among the attenders.

Statistical analysis was done after removing the dropout from the study.

Table 14, Graph 2: Age and Gender Distribution among Dentists

Dentist	Male		Female		Total	
	No	%	No		No	%
20-29	24	30	38	39.18	62	35.03
30-39	47	58.75	48	49.48	95	53.67
40-49	5	6.25	9	9.28	14	7.91
50-59	4	5	2	2.06	6	3.39
Total	80	100	97	100	177	100
Mean ± SD	33.09±6.39		32.14±6.32.		32.57±6.36	

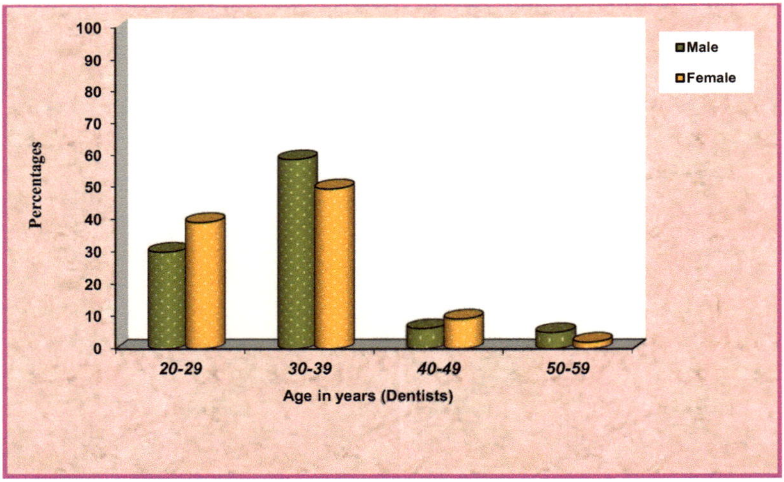

Table14, graph 2 shows the age and gender distribution of the dentist participated in the study. Among the 80 male dentists 24 %(n-30) were in the age group of 20-29 years, 58.7% (n-47) in 30-39 years, 6.25 %(n-5) in 40-49 years, 5 %

(n-4) in 50-59 years respectively. The mean age of male dentist was 33.09±6.39. Among the 97 female dentist 39.1 %(n-38) were in the age group of 20-29 years, 49.48% (n-48) in 30-39 years, 9.28 %(n-9) in 40-49 years, 2.06 %(n-2) in 50-59 years respectively. The mean age of female dentist was 32.14±6.32. Among 177 total dentists, 35.03 %(n-62) were in the age group of 20-29 years, 53.67% (n-95) in 30-39 years, 7.91 %(n-14) in 40-49 years, 3.39 %(n-6) in 50-59 years respectively with 32.57±6.36 mean age.

Table 15, Graph 3: Age and Gender Distribution among Auxiliaries

Auxiliary staff	Male		Female		Total	
	No	%	No	%	No	%
20-29	3	27.27	4	50	7	36.84
30-39	5	45.45	2	25	7	36.84
40-49	2	18.18	1	12.5	3	15.79
50-59	1	9.09	1	12.5	2	10.53
Total	11	100	8	100	19	100
Mean ± SD	35.00±7.72		33.88±9.43		34.53±8.2	

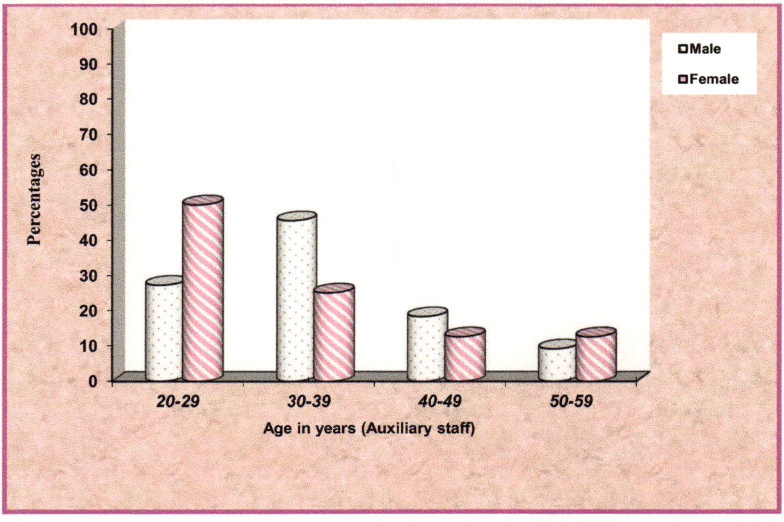

Table 15, graph 3 shows the age and gender distribution of the Auxiliaries participated in the study. Among the 11 male Auxiliaries, 27.27 %(n-3) were in the age group of 20-29 years, 45.45% (n-5) in 30-39 years, 18.18 %(n-2) in 40-49 years, 9.09 %(n-1) in 50-59 years respectively. The mean age for male auxiliaries was 35.00±7.72. Among the 8 female

Auxiliaries, 50%(n-4) were in the age group of 20-29 years, 25% (n-2) in 30-39 years, 12.5%(n-1) in 40-49 years, 12.5 %(n-1) in 50-59 years respectively. The mean age for female auxiliaries was 33.88±9.43. Among 19 total Auxiliaries, 36.8 %(n-7) were in the age group of 20-29 years, 36.84% (n-7) in 30-39 years, 15.79 %(n-3) in 40-49 years, 10.53 %(n-2)in 50-59 years respectively with 34.53±8.2 mean age.

Table 16, Graph 4: Age and Gender Distribution among attenders.

Age in years	Male		Female		Total	
	No	%	No	%	No	%
20-29	6	23.0	3	10.7	9	16.6
30-39	6	23.0	13	46.4	19	35.1
40-49	12	46.1	12	42.8	24	44.4
50-59	2	7.6	0	0.0	2	3.7
Total	26	100.0	28	100.0	54	100.0
Mean ± SD	37.15±7.46.		36.42±6.96		36.77±7.14.	

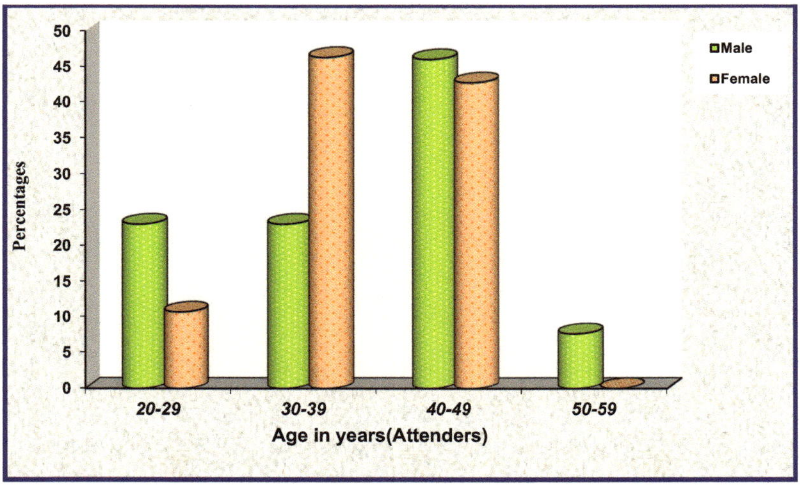

Table 16, graph 4 shows the age and gender distribution of the attenders participated in the study. Among the 26 male attenders, 23 %(n-6) were in the age group of 20-29 years, 23% (n-6) in 30-39 years, 46.1 %(n-12) in 40-49 years,7.6%(n-2) in 50-59 years respectively. The mean age of male attenders were 37.15±7.46. Among the 28 female attenders, 10.7%(n-3) were in the age group of 20-29 years, 46.4% (n-13) in 30-39 years, 42.8 %(n-12) in 40-49 years, respectively. The mean age of female attenders were 36.42±6.96. Among 54 total attenders, 16.6%(n-9) were in the age group of 20-29 years, 35.1% (n-19) in 30-39 years, 44.4 %(n-24) in 40-49 years, 3.7 %(n-2) in 50-59 years respectively with the mean age of 36.77±7.14.

Table 17, Graph 5: Evaluation of effect of training programme on knowledge (Correct response) regarding hospital waste management among the Dentists

Knowledge questions	Response	Pre-intervention (n=177)		Post-intervention (n=177)		% change	p value
		No	%	No	%		
Q1. Segregation of waste into different categories should be done at	The point of generation	**99**	**55.9**	**173**	**97.7**	**41.8**	**0.0002**
	The time of collection	20	11.3	0	0.0	-11.3	
	The time of treatment	5	2.8	1	0.6	-2.2	
	All the above	53	29.9	3	1.7	-28.2	
	Non response	0	0	0	0	0	
Q2. Disinfection before disposal helps to	Reduce the risk of transmission of infection	28	15.8	2	1.1	-14.7	
	Strengthen and support the overall standards of hospital hygiene	1	0.6	0	0.0	-0.6	
	Prevents the spread of multidrug- resistant and other nosocomial pathogen	2	1.1	1	0.6	-0.5	
	All of the above.	**144**	**81.4**	**174**	**98.3**	**16.9**	**0.045**
	Non response	2	1.1	0	0	0	
Q3. Identify the biohazard symbol		**123**	**69.5**	**174**	**98.3**	**28.8**	**0.001**
		0	0.0	0	0.0	0.0	
		2	1.1	0	0.0	-1.1	
		47	26.6	3	1.7	-24.9	
	Non response	5	2.8	0	0	0	
Q 4. Which of the following is not an acceptable technique for the handling of sharp needles?	Recapping a needle using a cap holder	14	7.9	1	0.6	-7.3	
	Recapping a needle using a "scoop technique"	5	2.8	1	0.6	-2.2	
	Disposing of a needle in general trash bag.	**147**	**83.1**	**175**	**98.9**	**15.8**	**0.068**
	Disposing of a needle in a puncture –resistant container	9	5.1	0	0.0	-5.1	

	Non response	2	1.1	0	0	0	
Q5. The presence of personal protective equipments	Prevents the transmission of infection from patient to dental health care personnel	9	5.1	1	0.6	-4.5	
	Prevents the transmission of infection from dental health care personnel to patient.	2	1.1	0	0.0	-1.1	
	Both of the above	**159**	**89.8**	**176**	**99.4**	**9.6**	**0.116**
	None of the above	4	2.3	0	0.0	-2.3	
	Non response	3	1.7	0	0		
Q6. The main risk posed by needle stick injury is exposure of the workers to blood- borne viruses	Hepatitis-B (HBV)	18	10.2	1	0.6	-9.6	
	Hepatitis-C (HCV)	0	0.0	0	0.0	0.0	
	Human immunodeficiency virus (HIV)	22	12.4	1	0.6	-11.8	
	All of the above	**134**	**75.7**	**176**	**99.4**	**23.7**	**0.007**
	Non response	3	1.7	0	0	0	
Q 7. Infectious waste is given the colour code of	Yellow	**115**	**65**	**175**	**98.9**	**33.9**	**0.000**
	Blue	30	16.9	2	1.1	15.8	
	Black	17	9.6	0	0.0	-9.6	
	Green	3	1.7	0	0.0	-1.7	
	Non response	12	6.8	0	0	0	
Q 8. Hepatitis-B immunization for health care	Not required	2	1.1	0	0.0	-1.14	
	May be given	2	1.1	0	0.0	-1.1	

workers	Compulsory	**171**	**96.6**	**177**	**100.0**	**3.4**	**0.352**
	Any of the above	1	0.6	0	0.0	-0.6	
	Non response	1	0.6	0	0	0	
Q9. After possible HIV exposure in health care worker	There is no risk of HIV transmission	6	3.4	1	0.6	-2.8	
	No immediate measure required	0	0.0	0	0.0	0.0	
	Post exposure prophylaxis to be initiated as soon as possible	**162**	**91.5**	**175**	**98.9**	**7.4**	**0.249**
	None of the above	6	3.4	1	0.6	-2.8	
	Non response	3	1.7	0	0	0	
Q10. Mercury and excess amalgam should be	Stored in water/ fixer solution	**158**	**89.3**	**177**	**100.0**	**10.7**	**0.143**
	Disposed in general trash	7	4.0	0	0.0	-4.0	
	Should be burnt	5	2.87	0	0.0	-2.8	
	Should be discharged in waste water.	4	2.3	0	0.0	-2.3	
	Non response	3	1.7	0	0	0	

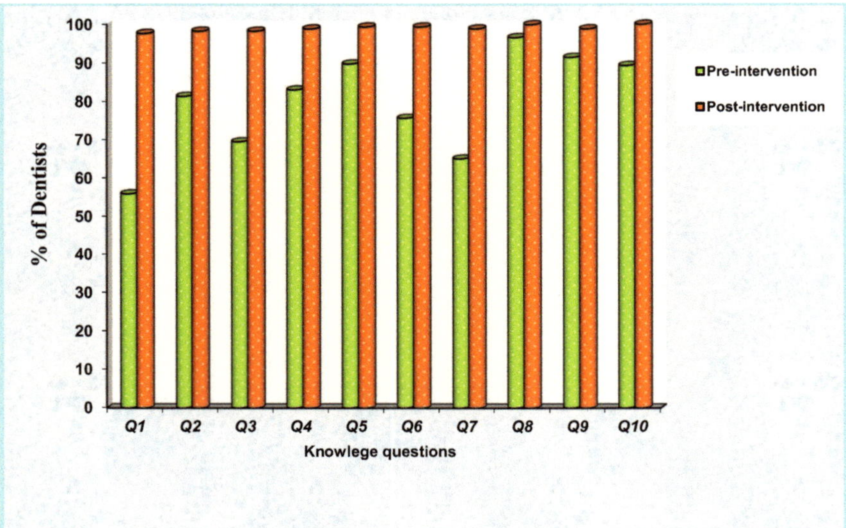

At baseline, 55.9% of dentist answered correctly, that Segregation of waste into different categories should be done at the point of generation. Post intervention there was increase in the correct response to 97.7%. Overall there was 41.8% ($p<.001$) improvement among the study group from the baseline.

At baseline, 81.4% of them answered correctly that the purpose of "Disinfection before disposal" reduce the risk of transmission of infection, strengthen and support the overall standards of hospital hygiene and also prevents the spread of multidrug- resistant and other nosocomial pathogen. After the intervention, 98.3% answered correctly, with the overall improvement of 16.9%. A total of 69.5% of dentist identified the biohazard symbol at the base line, and 28.8 % ($p<.001$) change was observed following intervention with 98.3% of dentist answering correctly.

With respect to the question regarding technique which is not acceptable for the handling of sharp needles, at baseline 83.1% of dentist answered correctly that disposing needle in general trash bag was not acceptable. After the intervention 98.9% answered correctly and there was 14.9 % improvement in the response. Question 5 assessed the participants' knowledge regarding personal protective equipments. 89.8%, 99.4% of the dentists answered correctly that personal protective equipments prevents the transmission of infection from patient to dental health care personnel and from dental health care personnel to patient at baseline and following intervention respectively with 9.6% change in the response.

A total of 75.7% of dentist knew that there could be risk posed to the workers by exposure of blood- borne viruses like Hepatitis-B (HBV), Hepatitis-C (HCV) Human immunodeficiency virus (HIV) with needle stick injury. 99.4% responded correctly after the intervention and the observed change in percentage from baseline was 23.7 % ($p<.001$).

When asked to identify the colour code for infectious waste yellow colour was correctly identified by 65% of dentist at baseline, and 98.9% following intervention with 33.9 % ($p<.001$)improvement in the response. 96.6 % of the dentist said that Hepatitis-B immunization for health care workers was compulsory at baseline, while 100% responded correctly after intervention with the overall change of 3.4 %.

A total of 91.5% responded correctly that post exposure prophylaxis should be initiated as soon as possible after possible HIV exposure in health care worker. There was 7.4 % change in the response following intervention with 98.9% answering correctly.

At baseline, 89.3 % of dentist knew that mercury and excess amalgam should be stored in water/ fixer solution. After intervention 100 % responded correctly and the observed change in percentage from baseline was 10.7 %.

Table 18, Graph 6: Evaluation of effect of training programme on attitude (Correct response) regarding waste management among the Dentists

Attitude questions	Response	Pre-intervention (n=177)		Post-intervention (n=177)		% change	P value
		No	%	No	%		
Q11. Segregation of waste at source increases the risk of injury to waste handlers	Strongly disagree	**59**	**33.3**	**164**	**92.7**	**59.4**	**0.0002**
	Disagree	53	29.9	7	4.0	-25.9	
	Don't know	9	5.11	5	2.8	-2.3	
	Agree	29	16.4	0	0.0	-16.4	
	Strongly agree	26	14.7	1	0.6	-14.1	
	Non response	1	0.6	0	0	0	
Q12. Decontamination / disinfection reduces chances of infection	Strongly disagree	3	1.71	0	0.0	-1.7	
	Disagree	0	0	0	0.0	0	
	Don't know	0	0	0	0.0	0	
	Agree	76	42.9	27	15.3	-27.6	
	Strongly agree	**96**	**54.2**	**150**	**84.7**	**30.5**	**0.0005**
	Non response	2	1.1	0	0	0	
Q13. Infectious waste should be put in yellow colored plastic bag with bio hazard symbol	Strongly disagree	6	3.4	0	0.0	-3.4	
	Disagree	3	1.7	0	0.0	-1.7	
	Don't know	2	1.7	0	0.0	-1.1	
	Agree	79	44.6	11	6.2	-38.4	
	Strongly agree	77	**43.5**	**166**	**93.8**	**50.3**	**0.0002**
	Non response	10	5.6	0	0	0	
Q14. Containment of sharps does not help in safe management of hospital waste	Strongly disagree	**48**	**27.1**	**155**	**87.6**	**60.5**	**0.0002**
	Disagree	65	36.7	18	10.2	-26.5	
	Don't know	14	7.9	1	0.6	-7.3	
	Agree	26	14.7	1	0.6	-14.1	
	Strongly agree	17	9.6	2	1.1	-8.5	

	Non response	7	4	0	0	0	
Q15. Occupational safety of waste handlers is a must	Strongly disagree	4	2.3	0	0.0	-2.3	
	Disagree	1	0.6	0	0.0	-0.6	
	Don't know	0	0.0	0	0.0	0.0	
	Agree	48	27.1	16	9.0	-18.1	
	Strongly agree	**121**	**68.4**	**161**	**91.0**	**22.6**	**0.007**
	Non response	3	1.7	0	0	0	
Q16. Reporting of needle stick injury is an extra burden on work.	Strongly disagree	**63**	**35.6**	**140**	**79.1**	**43.5**	**0.000**
	Disagree	71	40.1	30	16.9	-23.2	
	Don't know	11	6.2	3	1.7	-4.5	
	Agree	15	8.5	3	1.7	-6.8	
	Strongly agree	12	6.8	1	0.6	-6.2	
	Non response	5	2.8	0	0	0	
Q17. Use of colour code for segregation of waste is a must	Strongly disagree	3	1.7	0	0.0	-1.7	
	Disagree	1	0.6	0	0.0	-0.6	
	Don't know	0	0	0	0.0	-0	
	Agree	55	31.1	13	7.3	-23.8	
	Strongly agree	**117**	**66.1**	**164**	**92.7**	**26.6**	**0.002**
	Non response	1	0.6	0	0	0	
Q18. Hepatitis-B immunization prevents transmission of hospital acquired infection	Strongly disagree	10	5.6	0	0.0	-5.6	
	Disagree	28	15.8	6	3.4	-12.4	
	Don't know	4	2.3	4	2.3	0	
	Agree	77	43.5	23	13.0	-30.5	
	Strongly agree	**56**	**31.6**	**144**	**81.4**	**49.8**	**0.000**
	Non response	2	1.1	0	0	0	
Q19. Post exposure prophylaxis should be initiated as soon as possible	Strongly disagree	3	1.7	0	0.0	-1.7	
	Disagree	0	0.0	0	0.0	0.0	
	Don't know	1	0.5	0	0.0	-0.5	
	Agree	48	27.1	22	12.4	-14.7	
	Strongly agree	**122**	**68.9**	**155**	**87.6**	**18.7**	**0.020**

	Non response	3	1.7	0	0	0	
Q20. Excess mercury/ amalgam should be stored in water or fixer solution	Strongly disagree	4	2.3	0	0.0	-2.3	
	Disagree	3	1.7	0	0.0	-1.7	
	Don't know	0	0	0	0.0	0	
	Agree	66	37.3	22	12.4	-24.9	
	Strongly agree	**100**	**57.8**	**155**	**87.6**	**29.8**	**0.000**
	Non response	4	2.3	0	0	0	

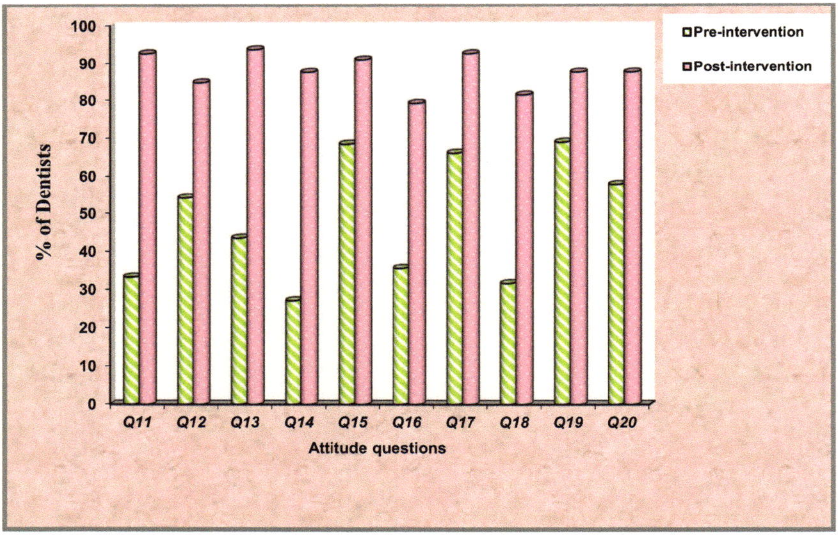

At baseline, 33.3% of dentist strongly disagreed that Segregation of waste at source increases the risk of injury to waste handlers. The response increased following intervention to 92.7% agreeing to it with overall 59.4 % change ($p<.001$). 54.2% of them strongly agreed decontamination / disinfection reduces chances of infection at baseline. And after intervention, 84.7% agreed to the same with 30.5% change ($p<.001$).

Before intervention 43.5% of dentist strongly agreed that Infectious waste should be put in yellow colored plastic bag, after intervention the response increased to 93.8% with overall change in 50.3 % ($p<.001$). 27.1% of dentist strongly disagreed to the statement

"Containment of sharps does not help in safe management of hospital waste" at baseline which increased to 87.6% after intervention with 60.5 % change ($p<.001$).

A total of 68.4% of dentist strongly agreed Occupational safety of waste handlers is a must before intervention. After intervention 91% agreed to the same with overall change of 22.6% ($p<.001$).At baseline, 35.6% of them strongly disagreed that reporting of needle stick injury is an extra burden on work. The response increased following intervention to 79.1% agreeing to it with overall 43.5 % change ($p<.001$).

66.1% of dentist strongly agreed use of colour code for segregation of waste is a must at baseline. And after intervention, 92.7% agreed to the same with 26.6% change ($p<.001$). Before intervention 31.6 % of them strongly agreed that Hepatitis-B immunization prevents transmission of hospital acquired infection after intervention the response increased to 46.6% with overall change in 49.8 %($p<.001$).

68.9% of dentist strongly agreed to the statement "Post exposure prophylaxis should be initiated as soon as possible" at baseline which increased to 87.6% after intervention with 18.7 % change. A total of 56.5% of dentist strongly agreed excess mercury/ amalgam should be stored in water or fixer solution before intervention. After intervention 87.6% agreed to the same with overall change of 29.8% ($p<.001$).

Table 19, Graph 7: Evaluation of effect of training programme on practice (Correct response) regarding hospital waste management among the Dentists

Practice questions	Response	Pre-intervention (n=177)		Post-intervention (n=177)		% change	P value
		No	%	No	%		
Q21. Do you segregate waste into different categories at the point of origin?	Yes	**146**	**82.5**	**170**	**96.0**	**13.5**	**0.081**
	No	30	16.4	7	4.0	-12.4	
	Non response	1	0.6	0	0	0	
Q22. Do you treat sharp waste prior to disposal?	Yes	**134**	**75.7**	**175**	**98.9**	**23.2**	**0.009**
	No	41	22.6	2	1.1	-21.5	
	Non response	2	1.1	0	0	0	
Q23. Do you dispose infectious waste in yellow colored plastic bag having biohazard symbol	Yes	**143**	**80.8**	**177**	**100.0**	**19.2**	**0.023**
	No	31	17.5	0	0.0	-17.5	
	Non response	3	1.7	0	0	0	
Q24. Do you use heavy duty (puncture proof) plastic container to collect the waste sharps ?	Yes	**127**	**71.8**	**177**	**100.0**	**28.2**	**0.001**
	No	47	26.6	0	0.0	-26.6	
	Non response	3	1.7	0	0	0	
Q25. Do you use personal protective devices? Apron	Yes	**171**	**96.6**	**177**	**100.0**	**3.4**	**0.352**
	No	2	1.1	0	0.0	-1.1	
	Non response	4	2.3	0	0	0	
	Yes	**175**	**98.9**	**177**	**100.0**	**1.1**	**0.425**
Mask	No	0	0	0	0.0	0	
	Non response	2	1.1	0	0	0	
	Yes	**174**	**98.8**	**177**	**100.0**	**1.2**	**0.425**
	No	0	0	0	0.0	-1.2	
	Non response	3	1.7	0	0	0	
Gloves	Yes	**123**	**69.5**	**175**	**98.9**	**29.4**	**0.001**
	No	42	23.7	2	1.1	-22.6	
	Non response	12	6.8	0	0	0	

Goggles							
Q26. Do you follow system of recording and reporting of injuries/accidents?	Yes	**111**	**62.7**	**162**	**91.5**	**28.8**	**0.001**
	No	58	32.8	15	8.5	-24.3	
	Non response	8	4.5	0	0	0	
Q27. Do you follow colour code for segregation of waste?	Yes	**148**	**83.6**	**175**	**98.9**	**15.3**	**0.068**
	No	25	14.1	2	1.1	-13.0	
	Non response	4	2.3	0	0	0	
Q28. Have you taken vaccination against hepatitis B?	Yes	**169**	**95.5**	**177**	**100.0**	**4.5**	**0.317**
	No	6	3.4	0	0.0	-3.4	
	Non response	2	1.1	0	0	0	
Q29. Following percutaneous exposure do you follow Post exposure prophylaxis?	Yes	**150**	**84.7**	**177**	**100.0**	**15.3**	**0.058**
	No	18	10.2	0	0.0	-10.2	
	Non response	9	5.1	0	0	0	
Q30. Do you store excess mercury/amalgam in water or fixer solution?	Yes	**143**	**80.8**	**173**	**97.7**	**16.9**	**0.044**
	No	28	15.8	4	2.3	-13.5	
	Non response	6	3.4	0	0	0	

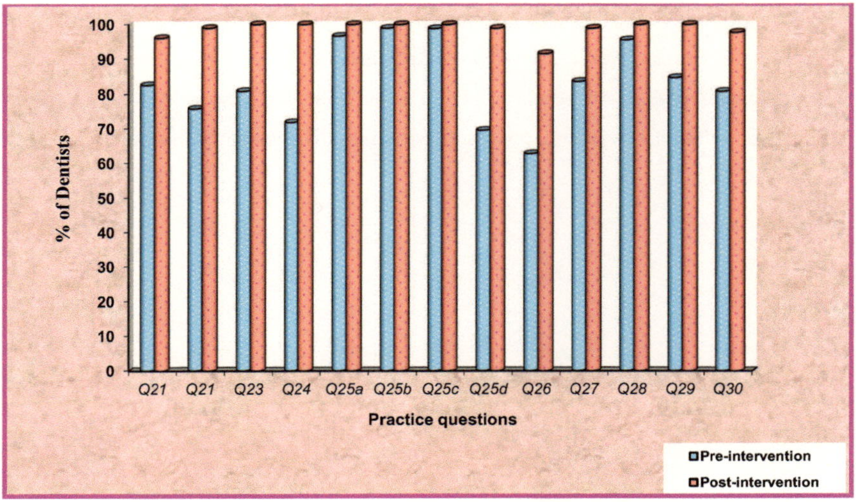

A total of 82.5% of dentist said that they segregate waste into different categories at the point of origin at baseline. Post intervention the response increased to 96% with overall change of 13.5%. At baseline, 75.7% of them responded yes for treating sharp waste prior to disposal. After intervention response increased to 98.9% with 23.2 % change (p<.001) from baseline.

80.8 % of dentist disposed infectious waste in yellow colored plastic bag having biohazard symbol at baseline; following intervention 100% responded the same, with 17.5% change. Before intervention 71.8% of them use heavy duty (puncture proof) plastic container to collect the waste sharps. There was a 28.2% change (p<.001) after intervention with response of 100%.

96.6% of respondents used Apron, 98.9% used mouth mask, 98.3% used gloves, and 69.5 % used goggles as personal protective devices at baseline, which increased to 100% after intervention with respect to apron, mask and gloves. With 98.9% increase in usage of goggles. 3.4%, 1.1%, 1.7%, 29.4% (p<.001) were overall change respectively for apron, mask, gloves and goggles respectively.

62.7% of dentist followed system of recording and reporting of injuries/accidents at the baseline, which increased to 91.5%, with 28.8 % (p<.001) overall change following the intervention. A total of 83.6 % of dentist followed colour code for segregation of waste at baseline. Post intervention the response increased to 98.9% with overall change 15.3 %.

At baseline, 95.5% of them had taken vaccination against hepatitis B, which increased to 100% after intervention with 4.5% change from baseline. Before intervention 84.7% of them followed post exposure prophylaxis following percutaneous exposure. There was a 15.3 % change after intervention with response of 100%. 80.8 % stored excess mercury/amalgam in water or fixer solution at baseline, post intervention the response increased to 97.7% with 16.0 % change.

Table 20, Graph 8: Evaluation of effect of training programme on knowledge (Correct response) regarding hospital waste management among the auxiliaries

Knowledge questions	Response	Pre-intervention (n=19)		Post-intervention (n=19)		% change	p value
		No	%	No	%		
Q1. Segregation of waste into different categories should be done at	The point of generation	**15**	**78.9**	**16**	**84.2**	**5.3**	**0.419**
	The time of collection	1	5.3	0	0.0	-5.3	
	The time of treatment	0	0.0	0	0.0	0.0	
	All the above	3	15.8	3	15.8	0.00	
	Non response	0	0	0	0	0	
Q2. Disinfection before disposal helps to	Reduce the risk of transmission of infection	1	5.6	0	0.0	-5.6	
	Strengthen and support the overall standards of hospital hygiene	0	0.0	0	0.0	0.0	
	Prevents the spread of multidrug- resistant and other nosocomial pathogen	0	0.0	0	0.0	0.0	
	All of the above.	**17**	**89.5**	**19**	**100**	**10.5**	**0.365**
	Non response	1	5.3	0	0	0	
Q3. Identify the biohazard symbol		**14**	**73.7**	**19**	**100.0**	**26.3**	**0.186**
		0	0.0	0	0.0	0.0	
		0	0.0	0	0.0	0.0	
		4	21.1	0	0.0	-21.1	
	Non response	1	5.3	0	0	0	
Q 4. Which of the following is not an acceptable technique for	Recapping a needle using a cap holder	1	5.3	2	10.5	5.2	
		0	0.0	1	5.3	5.4	

the handling of sharp needles?	Recapping a needle using a "scoop technique"						
	Disposing of a needle in general trash bag.	**16**	**84.2**	**16**	**84.2**	**0**	**0.500**
	Disposing of a needle in a puncture –resistant container	0	0.0	0	0.0	0.0	
	Non response	2	10.5	0	0	0	
Q5. The presence of personal protective equipments	Prevents the transmission of infection from patient to dental healthcare personnel	1	5.3	3	15.8	10.5	
	Prevents the transmission of infection from dental health care personnel to patient.	0	0.0	0	0.0	0.0	
	Both of the above	**15**	**78.9**	**16**	**84.2**	**5.3**	**0.419**
	None of the above	1	5.3	0	0.0	-5.8	
	Non response	2	10.5	0	0	0	
Q6. The main risk posed by needle stick injury is exposure of the workers to blood- borne viruses	Hepatitis-B (HBV)	1	5.3	0	0.0	-5.3	
	Hepatitis-C (HCV)	0	0.0	0	0.0	0.0	
	Human immunodeficiency virus (HIV)	2	10.5	0	0.0	-10.5	
	All of the above	**16**	**84.2**	**19**	**100.0**	**15.8**	**0.305**
	Non response	0	0	0	0	0	
Q 7. Infectious waste is given the colour code of	Yellow	**12**	**63.2**	**19**	**100.0**	**36.8**	**0.101**
	Blue	2	10.5	0	0.0	-10.5	
	Black	2	10.5	0	0.0	-10.5	
	Green	2	10.5	0	0.0	-10.5	
	Non response	1	5.3	0	0	0	
Q 8. Hepatitis-B immunization for health care workers	Not required	0	0.0	1	5.3	5.3	
	May be given	2	10.5	0	0.0	-10.5	

	Compulsory	**16**	**84.2**	**18**	**94.7**	**10.5**	**0.373**
	Any of the above	1	5.3	0	0.0	-5.3	
	Non response	0	0	0	0	0	
Q9. After possible HIV exposure in health care worker	There is no risk of HIV transmission	0	0.0	1	5.3	5.3	
	No immediate measure required	0	0.0	0	0.0	0.0	
	Post exposure prophylaxis to be initiated as soon as possible	**19**	**100.0**	**18**	**94.7**	**-5.3**	**0.426**
	None of the above	0	0.0	0	0.0	0.0	
	Non response	0	0	0	0	0	
Q10. Mercury and excess amalgam should be	Stored in water/ fixer solution	**10**	**52.6**	**18**	**94.7**	**42.1**	**0.062**
	Disposed in general trash	0	0.0	0	0.0	0.0	
	Should be burnt	8	42.1	0	0.0	-42.1	
	Should be discharged in waste water.	0	0.0	1	5.3	5.3	
	Non response	1	5.3	0	0	0	

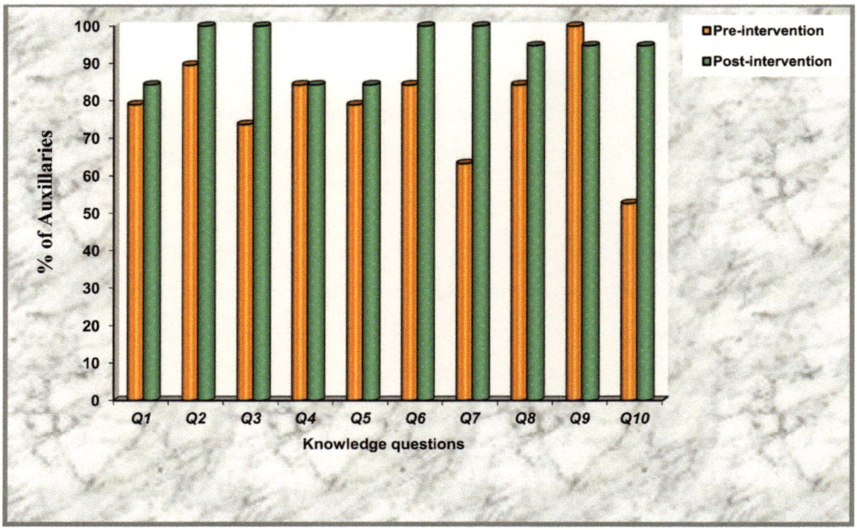

At baseline, with regards to the first question, 78.9% of auxiliaries answered correctly that Segregation of waste into different categories should be done at the point of generation. Post intervention there was increase in the correct response to 84.2%. Overall there was 5.3% improvement among the study group from the baseline.

At baseline, 89.5% of them answered correctly that the purpose of "Disinfection before disposal" reduce the risk of transmission of infection, strengthen and support the overall standards of hospital hygiene and also prevents the spread of multidrug- resistant and other nosocomial pathogen. After the intervention, 100% answered correctly, with the overall change of 10.5%. A total of 73.7 % of auxiliaries identified the biohazard symbol at the base line, and 26.3 % improvement was observed following intervention with 100% of auxiliary answering correctly.

With respect to the question regarding technique which is not acceptable for the handling of sharp needles, at baseline 84.2% of them answered correctly that disposing needle in general trash bag was not acceptable: With no change after the intervention from baseline.

Question 5 assessed the participants' knowledge regarding personal protective equipments. 78.9%, 84.2% of the auxiliaries answered correctly that personal protective equipments prevents the transmission of infection from patient to dental health care personnel and from dental health care personnel to patient at baseline and following intervention respectively with 5.3 % change in the response. A total of 84.2% of auxiliaries knew that there could be risk posed to the workers by exposure of blood- borne viruses like Hepatitis-B (HBV), Hepatitis-C (HCV) Human immunodeficiency virus (HIV) with needle stick injury. 100% responded correctly after the intervention and the observed improvement from baseline was 15.8 %

When asked to identify the colour code for Infectious waste 63.2%, 100% of auxiliaries correctly identified, yellow colour at baseline and following intervention respectively with 36.8 % improvement in the response. 84.2 % of the auxiliaries said that Hepatitis-B immunization for health care workers was compulsory at baseline, while 94.7 % responded correctly after intervention with the overall change of 10.5%.

A total of 100% of auxiliaries responded correctly that post exposure prophylaxis should be initiated as soon as possible after possible HIV exposure in health care worker. There were -5.3 % changes in the response following intervention with 94.7% answering correctly. At baseline, 52.6 % of them knew that mercury and excess amalgam should be Stored in water/ fixer solution. After intervention 94.7 % responded correctly and the observed improvement from baseline was 42.1 % ($p<.001$).

Table 21 , Graph 9 : Evaluation of effect of training programme on attitude (Correct response) regarding hospital waste management among the auxiliaries

Attitude questions	Response	Pre-intervention (n=19)		Post-intervention (n=19)		% change	P value
		No	%	No	%		
Q11. Segregation of waste at source increases the risk of injury to waste handlers	Strongly disagree	**12**	**63.1**	**16**	**84.2**	**21.0**	**0.226**
	Disagree	3	15.7	1	5.3	-10.4	
	Don't know	0	0.0	0	0.0	0.0	
	Agree	3	15.7	1	5.3	-10.4	
	Strongly agree	1	5.2	1	5.3	0.06	
	Non response	0	0	0	0	0	
Q12. Decontamination / disinfection reduces chances of infection	Strongly disagree	4	21.0	1	5.3	-15.7	
	Disagree	0	0	0	0.0	0	
	Don't know	0	0	0	0.0	0.0	
	Agree	4	21.0	3	15.8	-5.2	
	Strongly agree	**11**	**57.8**	**15**	**78.9**	**21.1**	**0.217**
	Non response	0	0	0	0	0	
Q13. Infectious waste should be put in yellow colored plastic bag with bio hazard symbol	Strongly disagree	1	5.2	1	5.3	0.1	
	Disagree	0	0	0	0.0	0	
	Don't know	0	0	0	0.0	0.0	
	Agree	6	31.5	0	0.0	-31.5	
	Strongly agree	**12**	**63.1**	**18**	**94.7**	**31.6**	**0.140**
	Non response	0	0	0	0	0	
Q14. Containment of sharps does not help in safe management of hospital waste	Strongly disagree	**3**	**15.7**	**14**	**73.7**	**58**	**0.001**
	Disagree	4	21.0	4	21.1	0.1	
	Don't know	0	0	0	0.0	0.0	

	Agree	6	31.5	1	5.3	-26.2	
	Strongly agree	6	31.5	0	0.0	-31.5	
	Non response	0	0	0	0	0	
Q15. Occupational safety of waste handlers is a must	Strongly disagree	1	5.3	1	5.3	0	
	Disagree	1	5.3	0	0.0	-5.3	
	Don't know	2	10.5	0	0.0	-10.5	
	Agree	5	26.3	2	10.5	-15.8	
	Strongly agree	**9**	**47.4**	**16**	**84.2**	**36.8**	**0.077**
	Non response	1	5.3	0	0	0	
Q16. Reporting of needle stick injury is an extra burden on work.	Strongly disagree	**8**	**42.1**	**14**	**73.7**	**31.6**	**0.102**
	Disagree	2	10.5	5	26.3	15.8	
	Don't know	1	5.2	0	0.0	-5.2	
	Agree	2	10.5	0	0.0	-10.5	
	Strongly agree	6	31.5	0	0.0	-31.5	
	Non response	0	0	0	0	0	
Q17. Use of colour code for segregation of waste is a must	Strongly disagree	4	21.0	1	5.3	-15.7	
	Disagree	3	15.7	0	0.0	-15.7	
	Don't know	1	5.2	0	0.0	-5.2	
	Agree	2	10.5	4	21.1	10.6	
	Strongly agree	**9**	**47.3**	**14**	**73.7**	**26.4**	**0.150**
	Non response	0	0	0	0	0	
Q18. Hepatitis-B immunization prevents transmission of hospital acquired infection	Strongly disagree	0	0.0	0	0.0	0.0	
	Disagree	0	0.0	1	5.3	5.2	
	Don't know	1	5.2	0	0.0	-5.2	
	Agree	4	21.0	2	10.5	-10.6	
	Strongly agree	**14**	**73.6**	**16**	**84.2**	**10.6**	**0.352**
	Non response	0	0	0	0	0	
Q19. Post exposure prophylaxis should be initiated as soon as possible	Strongly disagree	0	0.0	1	5.3	5.3	
	Disagree	0	0.0	0	0.0	0.0	
	Don't know	0	0.0	0	0.0	0.0	

	Agree	6	31.5	2	10.5	-21	
	Strongly agree	**13**	**68.4**	**16**	**84.2**	**15.8**	**0.287**
	Non response	0	0	0	0	0	
Q20. Excess mercury/ amalgam should be stored in water or fixer solution	Strongly disagree	0	0.0	1	5.3	5.3	
	Disagree	0	0.0	0	0.0	0.0	
	Don't know	0	0.0	0	0.0	0.0	
	Agree	5	26.3	3	15.8	-10.5	
	Strongly agree	**14**	**73.6**	**15**	**78.9**	**5.3**	**0.431**
	Non response	0	0	0	0	0	

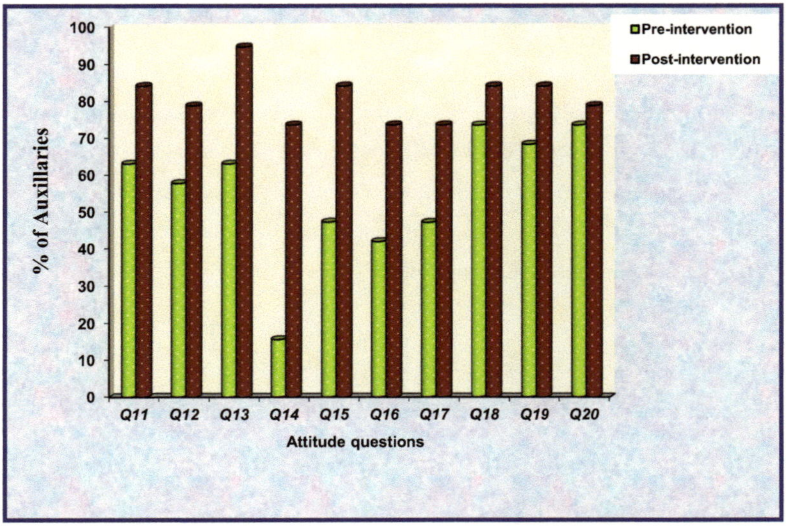

At baseline, 63.1% of auxiliaries strongly disagreed that Segregation of waste at source increases the risk of injury to waste handlers. The response increased following intervention to 84.2% agreeing to it with overall 21 % change. 57.8 % of them strongly agreed Decontamination / disinfection reduces chances of infection at baseline. And after intervention, 78.9 % agreed to the same with 21.1% change.

Before intervention 63.1% of them strongly agreed that Infectious waste should be put in yellow colored plastic bag, after intervention the response increased to 94.7% with overall change in 31.6 %. 15.7 % of auxiliaries strongly disagreed to the statement "Containment of sharps does not help in safe management of hospital waste" at baseline which increased to 73.7% after intervention with 58 % change ($p<.001$).

A total of 47.4 % of auxiliaries strongly agreed occupational safety of waste handlers is a must before intervention. After intervention 84.2% of them agreed to the same with overall change of 36.8 %($p<.001$). At baseline, 42.1% of auxiliaries strongly disagreed that reporting of needle stick injury is an extra burden on work. The response increased following intervention to 73.7% agreeing to it with overall 31.6 % change.

47.3% of them strongly agreed that use of colour code for segregation of waste is a must at baseline. And after intervention, 73.7% agreed to the same with 26.4% change. Before intervention 73.6% of auxiliaries strongly agreed that Hepatitis-B immunization prevents transmission of hospital acquired infection after intervention the response increased to 84.2% with overall change in 10.6 %.

68.4% of auxiliaries strongly agreed to the statement "Post exposure prophylaxis should be initiated as soon as possible" at baseline which increased to 84.2 % after intervention with 15.8% change. A total of 73.6% of auxiliaries strongly agreed Excess mercury/ amalgam should be stored in water or fixer solution before intervention. After intervention 78.9% agreed to the same with overall change of 5.3%.

Table 22, Graph 10: Evaluation of effect of training programme on practice (Correct response) regarding hospital waste management among the auxiliaries

Practice questions	Response	Pre-intervention (n=19)		Post-intervention (n=19)		% change	P value
		No	%	No	%		
Q21. Do you segregate waste into different categories at the point of origin?	Yes	**11**	**57.9**	**17**	**89.5**	**31.6**	**0.123**
	No	7	31.6	2	10.5	-21.1	
	Non response	1	5.3	0	0	0	
Q22. Do you treat sharp waste prior to disposal?	Yes	**15**	**78.9**	**16**	**84.2**	**5.3**	**0.419**
	No	4	21	3	15.8	-5.3	
	Non response	0	0	0	0	0	
Q23. Do you dispose infectious waste in yellow colored plastic bag having biohazard symbol	Yes	**14**	**73.7**	**19**	**100.0**	**26.3**	**0.186**
	No	4	21.1	0	0.0	-21.1	
	Non response	1	5.3	0	0		
Q24. Do you use heavy duty (puncture proof) plastic container to collect the waste sharps ?	Yes	**17**	**89.4**	**19**	**100.0**	**10.6**	**0.365**
	No	2	10.5	0	0.0	-10.6	
	Non response	0	0	0	0	0	
Q25. Do you use personal protective devices? Apron	Yes	**14**	**73.6**	**19**	**100.0**	**26.4**	**0.186**
	No	5	26.3	0	0.0	-26.4	
	Non response	0	0	0	0	0	
Mask	Yes	**18**	**94.7**	**18**	**94.7**	**0**	**0.500**
	No	1	5.2	1	5.3	-0.1	
	Non response	0	0	0	0	0	
	Yes	**19**	**100.0**	**19**	**100.0**	**0.0**	**0.500**
	No	0	0.0	0	0.0	0.0	
	Non response	0	0	0	0	0	
Gloves	Yes	**16**	**84.2**	**17**	**89.5**	**5.3**	**0.431**
	No	3	15.7	2	10.5	-5.3	
	Non response	0	0	0	0	0	

Goggles							
Q26. Do you follow system of recording and reporting of injuries/accidents?	Yes	**15**	**78.9**	**16**	**84.2**	**5.3**	**0.412**
	No	4	21.5	3	15.8	-5.3	
	Non response	0	0	0	0	0	
Q27. Do you follow colour code for segregation of waste?	Yes	**14**	**73.6**	**18**	**94.7**	**21.1**	**0.241**
	No	5	26.3	1	5.3	-21.1	
	Non response	0	0	0	0	0	
Q28. Have you taken vaccination against hepatitis B?	Yes	**17**	**89.4**	**19**	**100.0**	**10.6**	**0.365**
	No	2	10.5	0	0.0	-10.6	
	Non response	0	0	0	0	0	
Q29. Following percutaneous exposure do you follow Post exposure prophylaxis?	Yes	**18**	**94.7**	**19**	**100.0**	**5.3**	**0.426**
	No	1	5.2	0	0.0	-5.3	
	Non response	0	0	0	0	0	
Q30. Do you store excess mercury/amalgam in water or fixer solution?	Yes	**13**	**68.4**	**13**	**68.4**	**0**	**0.500**
	No	5	26.3	6	31.6	5.3	
	Non response	1	5.3	0	0	0	

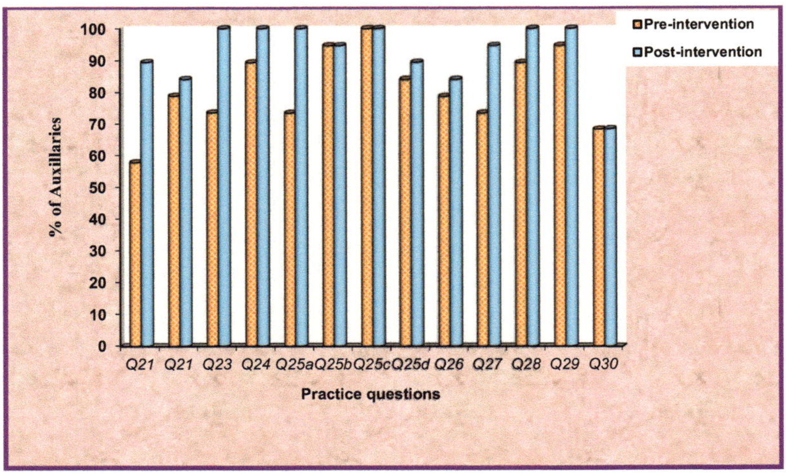

A total of 57.9% of auxiliaries said that they segregate waste into different categories at the point of origin at baseline. Post intervention the response increased to 89.5% with overall change of 31.4 %. At baseline, 78.9% of them responded yes for treating sharp waste prior to disposal. After intervention response increased to 84.2% with 5.3% change from baseline. 73.7% of them disposed infectious waste in yellow colored plastic bag having biohazard symbol at baseline; following intervention 100% responded the same, with 26.3 % change.

Before intervention 89.4% of auxiliaries use heavy duty (puncture proof) plastic container to collect the waste sharps. There was a 10.6% change after intervention with response of 100%. 73.6% of them used Apron at baseline, which increased to 100% after intervention with 26.4% change. 94.7% used mouth mask at baseline, with no change after intervention. All the respondents ie 100% used gloves as personal protective devices before and after intervention. 84.2% of them used goggles at baseline, which increased to 89.5% after intervention with 5.3% overall change.

78.9% of them followed system of recording and reporting of injuries/accidents at the baseline, which increased to 84.2%, with 5.3% overall change following the intervention. A total of 73.6% of auxiliaries followed colour code for segregation of waste at baseline. Post intervention the response increased to 94.7% with overall change 21.1%.

At baseline, 89.4% of them had taken vaccination against hepatitis B, which increased to 100% after intervention with 10.6 % change from baseline. Before intervention 94.7% followed Post exposure prophylaxis following percutaneous exposure. There was a 5.3% change after intervention with response of 100%. 68.4 % of them stored excess mercury/amalgam in water or fixer solution at baseline, post intervention there was no change.

Table 23, Graph 11: Evaluation of effect of training programme on knowledge (Correct response) regarding hospital waste management among the attenders

Knowledge questions	Response	Pre-intervention (n=54)		Post-intervention (n=54)		% change	P value
		No	%	No	%		
Q1. Identify the biohazard symbol		**33**	**61.1**	**50**	**92.6**	**31.5**	**0.031**
		-	-	-	-	-	
		-	-	-	-	-	
		12	22.2	4	7.4	-14.8	
	Non response	9	16.7	0	0	0	
Q2. Infectious waste should be disposed of in which the colour code bag	Yellow	**39**	**72.2**	**47**	**87.1**	**14.9**	**0.191**
	Blue	10	18.5	7	12.9	-5.6	
	Black	5	9.2	-	-	-9.2	
	Greeen	0	0.0	-	-	0.0	
	Non response	0	0	0	0	0	

Q3. Exposure to needle stick injury to workers may cause which disease	Hepatitis-B (HBV)	3	5.5	2	3.7	-1.8	
	Hepatitis-C (HCV)	1	1.8	-	-	-1.8	
	Human immunodeficiency virus (HIV)	22	40.7	7	12.9	-27.8	
	All of the above	**28**	**51.8**	**45**	**83.3**	**31.5**	**0.019**
	Non response	0	0	0	0	0	
Q4. Should you use personal protective devices while handling hospital waste?	Yes	**51**	**94.4**	**54**	**100.0**	**5.6**	0.376
	No	0	0.0	0	0.0	0	
	Non response	3	5.6	0	0	0	
Apron	Yes	**47**	**87.0**	**50**	**92.6**	**5.6**	0.392
	No	4	7.4	4	7.4	0	
	Non response	3	5.6	0	0	0	
Gloves	Yes	**42**	**77.8**	**51**	**94.4**	**16.6**	0.170
	No	7	13	3	5.6	-7.4	
	Non response	5	9.3	0	0	0	
Mask							
Q5 Disposing needle and waste sharps in general trash bag is a safe procedure	Yes	10	18.5	6	11.1	-7.5	
	No	**44**	**81.4**	**48**	**88.9**	**7.5**	0.341
	Non response	0	0	0	0	0	

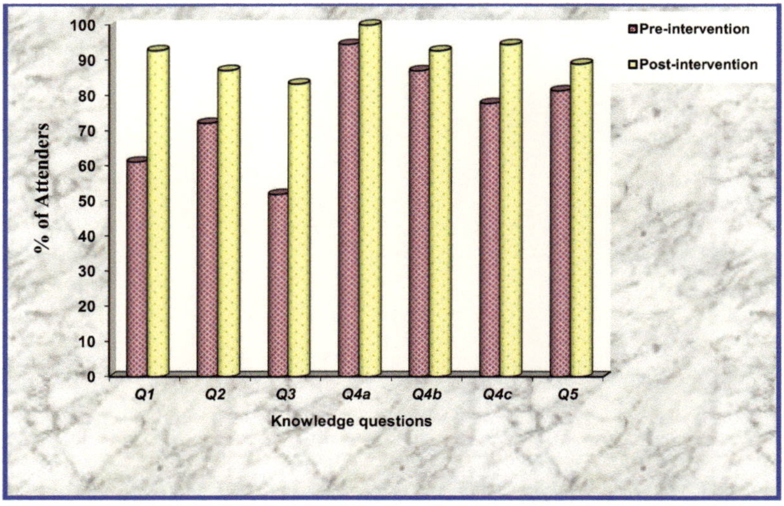

A total of 61.1% of participants identified the biohazard symbol at the base line, and 31.5 % improvement ($p<.001$) was observed following intervention with 92.6 % of them answering correctly. At baseline 72.2% of attenders knew Infectious waste should be disposed of in yellow colour code bag. Following intervention, 87.1% of them answered correctly, with 14.9 % overall change from baseline.

51.8% of attenders correctly identified the disease caused by exposure to needle stick injury at baseline, and 31.5% improvements was observed with 83.3% response following intervention. A total of 94.4%, 87%, and 77.8% of respondents knew apron, gloves, mouth mask should be used as a personal protective device while handling hospital waste respectively at baseline. After intervention 100%, 92.6%, 94.4% of them started to use personal protective device with 5.6%, 5.6% and 16.6% change respectively. 81.4% of them knew disposing needle and waste sharps in general trash bag is not a safe procedure at baseline. Following intervention, 88.9% of them answered correctly with 7.5% change from baseline.

Table 24, Graph 12: Evaluation of effect of training programme on attitude (Correct response) regarding hospital waste management among the attenders

Attitude questions	Response	Pre-intervention (n=54)		Post-intervention (n=54)		% change	P value
		No	%	No	%		
Q6. Is it necessary to segregate waste into different categories at the point of origin	Yes	**46**	**85.1**	**52**	**96.3**	**11.2**	**0.274**
	No	8	14.8	2	3.7	-11.2	
	Non response	0	0	0	0	0	
Q7. Reporting of needle stick injury is an extra burden on work.	Yes	40	74.1	15	27.8	-46.3	
	No	**9**	**16.7**	**39**	**72.2**	**55.5**	**0.0002**
	Non response	5	9.3	0	0	0	
Q8. Segregation of waste at source increases the risk of injury to waste handlers	Yes	24	44.4	16	29.6	-14.8	
	No	**28**	**51.9**	**38**	**70.4**	**18.5**	0.101
	Non response	2	3.7	0	0	0	
Q9. Is it necessary to take vaccination against hepatitis B	Yes	**32**	**59.2**	**47**	**87.0**	**27.8**	**0.043**
	No	22	40.7	7	13.0	-27.8	
	Non response	0	0	0	0	0	
Q10. Hepatitis-B immunization prevents transmission of hospital acquired infection	Yes	**30**	**55.5**	**43**	79.6	**24.1**	**0.062**
	No	24	44.4	11	20.3	-24.1	
	Non response	0	0	0	0	0	

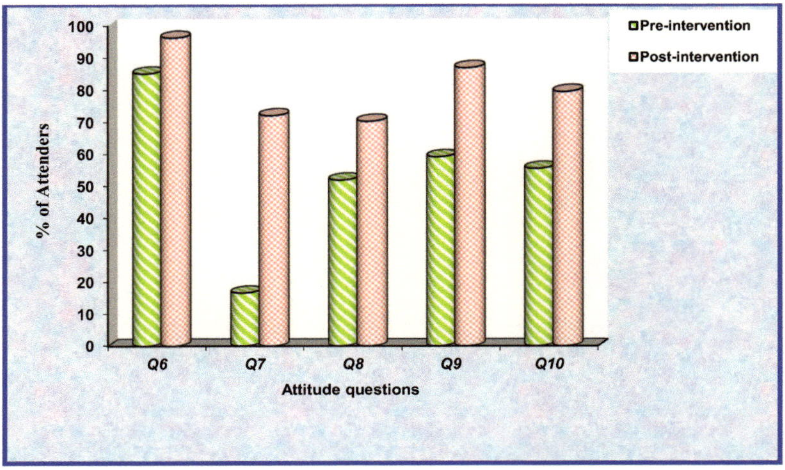

85.1% of attenders said it necessary to segregate waste into different categories at the point of origin. After intervention the response increased to 96.3% with a change of 11.2% from baseline. A total of 16.7% of attenders said reporting of needle stick injury is not an extra burden on work at baseline. Post intervention, 72.2% agreed to the same with 53.9% change ($p<.001$) from baseline.

At baseline 51.9 % of them agreed that Segregation of waste at source does not increases the risk of injury to waste handlers. Following intervention the response increased to 70.4% with overall 18.5% change from baseline. 59.2% felt it is necessary to take vaccination against hepatitis B, at baseline. Post intervention the response increased to 87% with 27.8% change from baseline. Before intervention, 55.5% of attenders agreed that Hepatitis-B immunization prevents transmission of hospital acquired infection. The response increased following intervention to 79.6% agreeing to it with overall 24.1% change.

Table 25, Graph 13: Evaluation of effect of training programme on practice (Correct response) regarding hospital waste management among the attenders

Practice questions	Response	Pre-intervention (n=54)		Post-intervention (n=54)		% change	P value
		No	%	No	%		
Q11. Do you segregate waste into different categories at the point of origin?	Yes	**49**	**90.7**	**50**	**92.6**	**1.9**	**0.456**
	No	5	9.2	4	7.4	-1.8	
	Non response	0	0	0	0	0	
Q12. Do you use personal protective devices? Apron	Yes	**50**	**92.6**	**50**	**92.6**	**0.0**	**0.500**
	No	1	1.9	4	7.4	5.5	
	Non response	3	5.6	0	0	0	
Gloves	Yes	**50**	**92.6**	**47**	**87.0**	**-5.6**	**0.392**
	No	1	1.9	7	13.0	11.1	
	Non response	3	5.6	0	0	0	
Mask	Yes	**43**	**79.6**	**49**	**90.7**	**11.1**	**0.267**
	No	5	9.3	5	9.3	0.0	
	Non response	6	11.1	0	0	0	
Q13. Do you dispose infectious waste in yellow colored plastic	Yes	**51**	**94.4**	**52**	**96.3**	**1.9**	**0.457**
	No	3	5.5	2	3.7	-1.9	
	Non response	0	0	0	0	0	
Q14. Do you follow system of recording and reporting of injuries/accidents?	Yes	**18**	**33.3**	**18**	**33.3**	**0**	**0.500**
	No	35	64.8	36	66.7	1.9	
	Non response	1	1.9	0	0	0	
Q15. Have you taken vaccination against hepatitis B?	Yes	**14**	**25.9**	**16**	**29.6**	**3.7**	**0.345**
	No	40	74.0	38	70.4	-3.7	
	Non response	0	0	0	0	0	

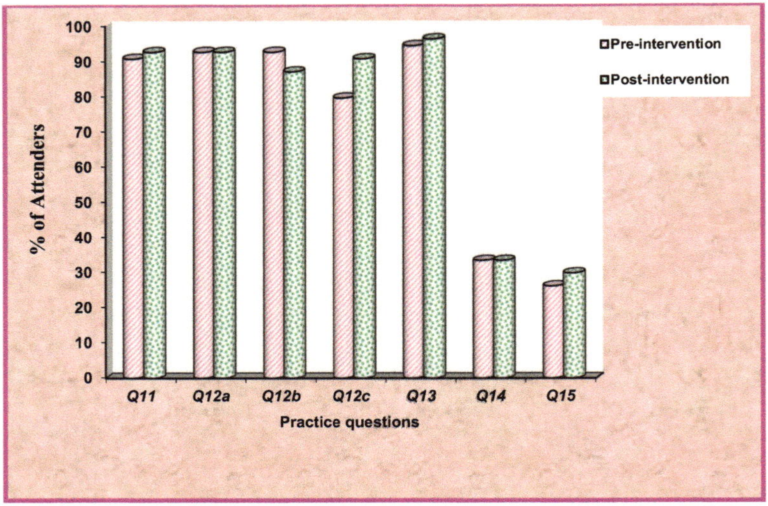

A total of 90.7% of attenders said that they segregate waste into different categories at the point of origin at baseline. Post intervention the response increased to 92.6% with overall change of 1.9%. 92.6% of attenders used Apron at baseline, with no change after intervention. 92.6% of them used gloves at baseline, which decreased to 87% after intervention with -5.6 % overall change. 79.6% used mouth mask at baseline, which increased to 90.7% after intervention with 11.1 % overall change.

94.4% of attenders disposed infectious waste in yellow colored plastic bag at baseline; following intervention 96.3% responded the same, with 1.9% change. 33.3% of them followed system of recording and reporting of injuries/accidents at the baseline, with no change following the intervention. At baseline, 25.9% had taken vaccination against Hepatitis B, which increased to 29.6% after intervention with 3.7% change from baseline.

Table 26, Graph 14: Evaluation of Knowledge, Attitude and Practice among Dentist

Score	Pre-intervention	Post-Intervention	Significance	% Change	Effect size
Knowledge score	7.95±1.74	9.89±0.36	<0.001**	24.4%	1.84(VL)
Attitude score	35.72±4.22	48.64±1.51	<0.001**	36.2%	4.51(VL)
Practice	10.86±2.26	12.77±0.77	<0.001**	17.6%	1.26(VL)

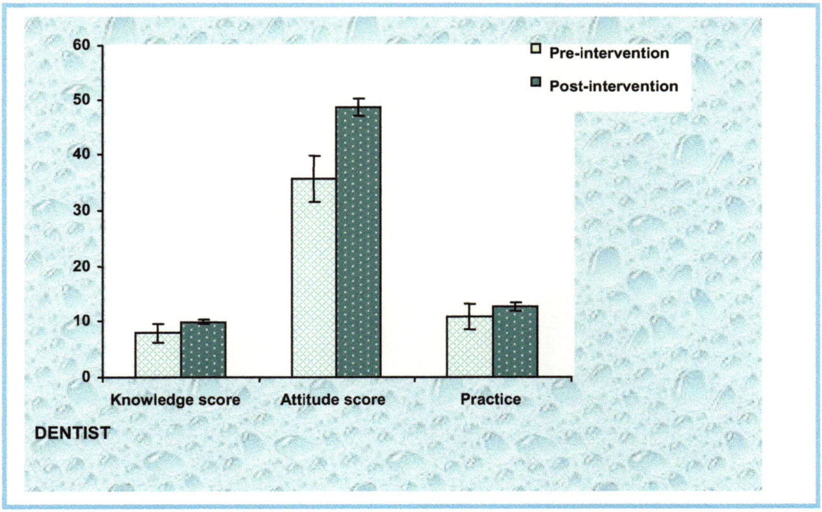

The mean Knowledge score was 7.95±1.74 at baseline, increased to 9.89±0.36 after intervention, which was statistically significant (P≤0.001) with a very large effect size of 1.84 with overall improvement in knowledge of 24.4%. The mean attitude score was 35.72±4.22 at baseline, increased to 48.64±1.51 after intervention, which was statistically significant (P≤0.001) with a very large effect size of 4.51 and overall 36.2% change in attitude. The mean practice score was 10.86±2.26 at baseline, increased to 12.77±0.77 after intervention, which was statistically significant (P≤0.001) with a large effect size of 1.26 with overall change of 17.6% in practice.

Table 27, Graph 15: Evaluation of Knowledge, Attitude and Practice in among auxiliaries

Score	Pre-intervention	Post-Intervention	Significance	% Change	Effect size
Knowledge score	7.89±1.82	9.37±1.17	0.010*	18.7%	0.99(L)
Attitude score	35.53±3.78	47.11±5.74	<0.001**	33.3%	2.43(VL)
Practice	10.58±2.61	12.32±0.82	0.017*	16.4%	1.01(L)

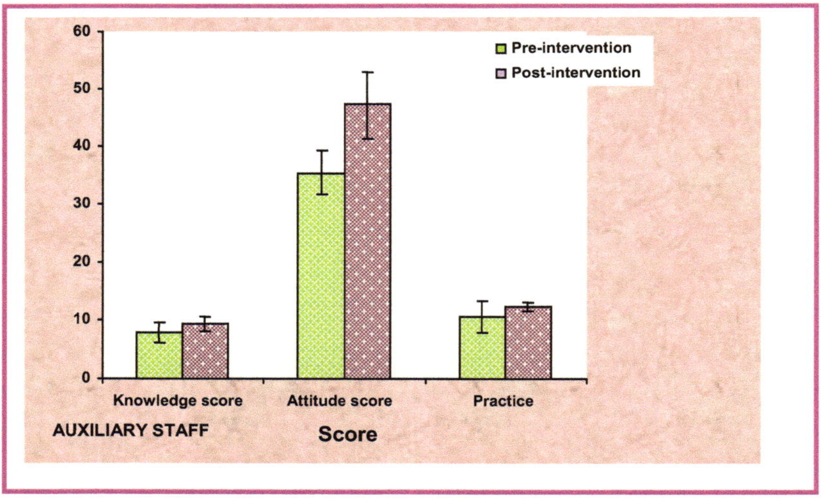

The mean knowledge score was 7.89±1.82 at baseline, increased to 9.37±1.17 after intervention, which was statistically significant (P≤0.01) with a large effect size of 0.99 with overall 18.7% improvement in knowledge.. The mean attitude score was 35.53±3.78 at baseline, increased to 47.11±5.74 after intervention, with a large effect size of 2.43 and 33.3% change in attitude. The mean practice score was 10.58±2.61 at baseline, increased to 12.32±0.82 after intervention, which was statistically significant (P≤0.01) with a large effect size of 1.01 with the overall change of 16.4% in practice.

Table 28, Graph 16: Evaluation of Knowledge, Attitude and Practice in among attenders

Score	Pre-intervention	Post-Intervention	Significance	% Change	Effect size
Knowledge score	5.03±1.64	6.27±1.09	<0.001**	23.3%	0.91 (L)
Attitude score	2.57±1.12	4.02±1.04	<0.001**	56.4%	1.34(VL)
Practice	5.00±0.87	5.22±1.18	0.546	4.4%	0.21(S)

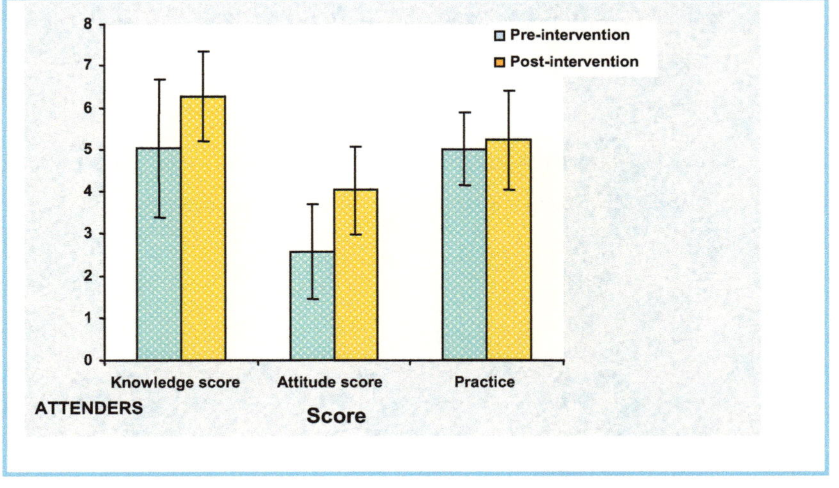

The mean knowledge score was 5.03±1.64 at baseline, increased to 6.27±1.09 after intervention, which was statistically significant (P≤0.01) with a large effect size of. 0.91, and overall improvement in knowledge of 23.3%. The mean attitude score was 2.57±1.12 at baseline, increased to 4.02±1.04 after intervention, with a very large effect size of 1.34 and overall change of 56.4% in attitude. The mean practice score was 5.00±0.87 at baseline, increased to 5.22±1.18 after intervention, which was not statistically significant with a small effect size of 0.21 and 4.4% change in practice.

Table 29, 30: CHECK LIST EVALUATION

The waste management practices were observed and documented using a check list before and after the intervention. Check list was used in the study to check the authenticity of the information given by the participants by the way of questionnaire. Names of the dental teaching hospitals are kept confidential. Among the eight dental teaching hospitals only 25% of these hospitals segregate waste at the point of origin. And 12.5% follow colour code for segregation. None of the hospitals treat waste sharps prior to disposal. All the hospitals have leak resistant Containers with tight fitting lids. Display of standard operating protocols for hospital waste management is followed by only 37.5% of the hospitals. 37.5% hospitals follow Occupational safety of waste handlers by using uniform, gloves, mask, goggles. None of the hospitals follow the system of recording and reporting of injuries/accidents during waste handling. Waste is stored in a secure area to deny unauthorized person's access and to protect against natural elements in all the hospitals. In all the hospitals waste is picked up by licensed haulers for transport to a licensed treatment facility. Recyclable materials like fixer, lead foil, and excess amalgam are sold to a suitable buyer or agency in all the hospitals.

When the researcher personally visited the various departments in the hospitals, there was no change in the waste management practices after the training programme when compared to baseline.

DISCUSSION

Hospitals and other health-care establishments have a "duty of care" for the environment and for public health, and have particular responsibilities in relation to the waste they produce. It is ironical that the very hospital that brings relief to the sick can create health hazard for hospital staff, patients as well as the community at large. Safe management of health care waste becomes very important when it comes to environment conservation and health of the community. The onus is on such establishments to ensure that there are no adverse health and environmental consequences of their waste handling, treatment, and disposal activities.

The concern regarding the biomedical waste is mainly due to the presence of pathogenic organisms and organic substances having adverse effect over human health. There could be significant number of organisms in the waste including virulent strains of viruses and pathogenic bacteria. Apart from the risk of water, air and soil pollution, it has considerable impact on human health due to aesthetic effects and threat to environmental health as suggested by Qureshi Waseem etal[21]

The awareness about global pollution has increased over the years and "Save the Earth" programmes have gained prime importance. It has led to the awareness that certain methods of disposal of such waste pose a great risk to the human health and the quality of environment. This has prompted hospital administrators to seek ever safe and cost-effective ways of scientific approach towards handling and managing hospital wastes.

Most waste generated in healthcare establishments can be treated as regular solid municipal waste as reported by Lars M. Johannessen[27], et.al. But a varying proportion of Health care waste requires special attention, including sharps (e.g. needles, razors, and scalpels), pathological waste, other potentially infectious waste, pharmaceutical waste, biological waste, and hazardous chemical waste.

According to World Health Organization[1], "The human's element is more important than the technology. Almost any system of treatment and disposal that is operated by well – trained, and well –motivated staff can provide more protection for staff, patients and the community than an expensive or sophisticated system that is managed by staff who do not understand the risks, and the importance of their contribution".

For effective management of hospital waste it is essential that personnel hold positive attitude towards care of the environment, occupational health and safety and teamwork. It will be apt to remember recommendations of WHO ***"human element is more important than technology".*** Hospital waste management has major attitudinal and behavioural components.

Literature search show poor knowledge, attitude and practices of biomedical waste management among staff and have reported that there is urgent need to train and educate all the staff, in order to adopt an effective waste management practice. A chain is as strong as the weakest link in it, thus the entire staff involved in waste management at some point or the other should be trained properly.

Studies [9,11,14] have suggested extensive training programmes for staff will surely help in changing their attitude and behaviour for the effective implementation of hospital waste management, which should be supplemented by periodic monitoring, supervision and motivation.

Saraf. Y. etal[17] have reported which showed improvement in the knowledge and practices among the staff after a training programme jointly organized by Medical College & Center for Pollution Control Board regarding hospital waste management.

It was observed that a training programme that includes redefining biomedical waste, reviewing waste practices throughout the hospital, educating staff and considering monetary outcomes could decrease amount of biomedical waste within few months.

Before providing the training programme, it is mandatory to understand the existing gaps and deficiencies in the study participants' knowledge, perceptions, behaviour towards hospital waste management. Knowledge, attitude and practices of the personnel play an important role. Because the lack of these even with good infrastructure and technology is of little or no use in proper waste management. Knowing this, the training programme can be aimed to make participants understand- environment friendly, healthy and economically viable in-house management systems, to ensure that the waste is carried responsibly from cradle to grave.

So, in this view, an interventional study, first of its kind was conducted to assess the knowledge, attitude and practice about hospital waste management and a training programme was provided for the staff on hospital waste management and effectiveness of training programme was assessed among the staff of dental teaching hospitals in Bangalore city. Since, there is scarcity of literature available with respect to assessment of effectiveness of training programme on hospital waste management; the comparative analysis could not be done appropriately.

For the purpose of conducting this study cluster sampling procedure was adopted, and eight dental teaching hospitals were randomly selected considering the constraints of limited resources like manpower, finance, and administrative logistics. All the staff of dental teaching hospitals willing to participate i.e dentists, dental auxiliary, attenders were included in the study. Staffs directly or indirectly not involved in hospital waste generation were excluded.

Though several attempts were made to involve each and every participant, still it was not possible to enroll all of them for the training programme. 177 dentists, 19 auxiliaries and 54 attenders completed the study. And the dropouts were 31.6% of dentists, 26.9% of the auxiliaries and 21.7% of the attenders.

In the present study, 75.7% of dentists were aware of risk posed by needle stick injury before intervention. Where as in a study conducted by Kishore J [9] et al, it was observed not all dentists were aware of the risks they were exposed to. 99.4% of dentists became aware of the risk after intervention in the present study.

In the present study 65% of the dentists reported rightly that the yellow bag should be used for infected waste. Kishore J [9]et al have reported 28% of the dentists have identified yellow bag should be used for infected waste.

In the present study, 43.4% of the attenders were aware that they were at risk to get fatal infections like HIV, HBV, and HCV. This observation was less when compared to study done by Saraf. Y. etal[17] which reported 54% of the attenders were aware about the same.

In the present study 98.6% of dentists were using apron, mask and gloves as personal protection devices for infection control. This finding was more when compared to study done by Treasure E et al[7] (94.5% gloves, 83.4 % masks) and Kishore[9] J et al (67% gloves). The reason for this was stated as insufficient supply of gloves in the hospital in the study done by Kishore[9] J et al.

In the present study, 80.8% of dentists used biohazard symbol for infectious waste which was high when compared to study done by Joseph J et al[13] which reported only 15%. In the present study, 62.7% of dentists reported that they maintain a register for injury/ accident reporting, which is high when compared to study done by Joseph J et al[13] which reported only 9% of dentist maintaining it .

Within hospitals, maintaining injury records/ register are important tools as they provide a basis for introducing control measures. It helps in assessing the efficacy of those control measures taken by the establishment, in reducing the level of avoidable infection. It will also ensure that the control measures have maximum effect and are as cost effective as possible.

In the present study, 83.6% of dentists followed colour coding which was high when compared to study done by Joseph J et al[13] which reported 26% of dentist following it.

In the present study 80.8% of dentists stored waste/excess amalgam in water this finding was high when compared to other studies by Treasure E et al[7] (62.6%) and Sudhakar V[11] et al (60.9%).

In the present study, 4.5 % were not immunized against Hepatitis B. The findings were less compared to the findings of Joseph J[13] etal (16 %) which reported that immunization coverage was observed to be less which could be because of high cost.

In the present study 71.8 % of dentists reported that they use puncture proof containers for disposal of waste sharps. This observation is high compared to the findings in the study done by Darwish RO[10] et al (13.5%).

In the present study 82.5% of dentists, reported that they segregated waste at the point of generation. Segregation practices in the present study among dentists were more when compared to the studies done by Joseph, J. et al (24%) and Sudhakar V et al (64.3%).

Proper segregation, containment, and disposal of dental hospital waste were not being carried out in hospitals surveyed by Nazar MW[28] et al. Quantitative information related to disposal of hazardous waste indicated that dental clinics disposed off bloody swabs into the waste paper bin ,contaminated sharps items into the general house hold refuse collection. Pandit NA[29] et al revealed that waste management process, segregation and storage were not properly followed. However, collection and transportation activities to final disposal were being practiced.

Sibusiso Derrick[30] et al also reported that inappropriate segregation practices are the dominant problem, which led to increased quantities of generated infectious waste and hence higher costs for its disposal.

Segregation could be described as an appropriate technology for waste management and it in many ways is the ***heart, soul,*** **and** ***mind*** of any system of waste management.

One days training programme was organized at each dental teaching hospital. Training programme covered the following aspects: importance of need to manage the waste in hospitals, the various aspects of management like segregation, disinfection, colour coding and clearly identifying each ones roles and responsibilities .

And also, the training programmes should be conducted more frequently because generally the staff turnover rate in the hospital is quite high. So, there should be ongoing training to ensure the new staff knows about this, besides being a continuous reminder for old staff.

Two months after the training programme, the overall evaluation of knowledge, attitude and practice among the staff showed a 24.4% improvement in the knowledge among the dentists, 18.7% improvement among auxiliaries ($p<0.001$, significant) and 23.3% improvements among the attenders when compared to the baseline knowledge. And there was 36.2% change in attitude among the dentists, 33.3% change among auxiliaries, and 56.42% and among the attenders ($p<0.001$, significant) when compared to the baseline attitude. There was a change of 17.6% in practice among the dentists, 16.4% change among auxiliaries, and 4.4 % among the attenders when compared to the baseline practice.

It was seen that greater percentage of questions were answered correctly after training programme when compared to baseline among all the study groups. The training programme enhanced knowledge, changed attitude and practices among the staff to achieve the desired objectives. But, this change can sustain in long term with good administration and organization, requires adequate legislation and financing.

The researcher personally visited the departments to check the authenticity of the information given by the respondents by the way of questionnaires. However, when authenticities of these responses were checked by the investigator there was complete mismanagement of hospital waste in these hospitals. There was no change in the waste management practices after the training programme when compared to baseline practices. Omissions and negligence at every stage of the waste management system was observed. There was lack of involvement from the hospital administration and so there was not much change observed in practice though the practice questions were answered correctly after training.

Among the eight dental teaching hospitals only 25 %(n-2) of these hospitals segregates waste at the point of origin. And 12.5 %(n-1) follow colour code for segregation. None of the hospitals treat waste sharps prior to disposal. All the hospitals have leak resistant Containers with tight fitting lids. Display of standard operating protocols for hospital waste management is followed by only 37.5% (n-3) of the hospitals. 37.5% (n-3) hospitals follow Occupational safety of waste handlers by using uniform, gloves, mask, and goggles. None of the hospitals follow the system of recording and reporting of injuries/accidents during waste handling. Waste is stored in a secure area to deny unauthorized person's access and to protect against natural elements in all the hospitals (n-8). In all the hospitals (n-8) waste is picked up by licensed haulers for transport to a licensed treatment facility. Recyclable materials like fixer, lead foil, and excess amalgam are sold to a suitable buyer or agency in all the hospitals (n-8)

It is very discouraging to know that current status of management of hospital waste in these hospitals does not fulfill the requirements of BMW rules.

Health-care waste management is strongly influenced by cultural, social, and economic circumstances. Experts working in this field opine that waste management committee should be formed which would be helpful in overseeing the day to day activities concerning waste management. The head of the hospital should form a waste management team to develop a waste management plan and should formally appoint the members of the waste management team in writing, informing each of them of their duties and responsibilities. The waste management team should review annually and initiate changes necessary to upgrade the waste management system. Interim revisions may also be made as and when necessary.

Hence, a well designed hospital waste policy, a legislative framework, and plans for achieving local implementation are essential.

Optimal waste management is at best, a moving target. Usually attenders are responsible for spearheading the waste management initiatives. Waste-handling is left to lower-level workers who operate without any training, guidance, and supervision. Managing waste requires the effective management of the people who produce the waste, not just those who handle it. It's primarily the dentists who are responsible for waste generation. But currently, as most of us are aware it is mainly the resistant attitude of dentists that is responsible for poor results on this front. Dentist at the high end of hierarchy should take this issue which needs to be addressed not as a burden difficult to bear. Proper management of dental hospital waste should be addressed with dignity, by concerted action as duty, and by no uncertain terms as responding to pressure. They probably should not do it because there is legislation, but they need to do it as they are socially accountable.

An improvement in hospital waste management involves a number of activities, which can be undertaken as series of small steps on the road to improvement. There is no 'one stop' technical solution. Spending money on impressive machinery does not guarantee an improvement. Improvement results from training, provision of storage equipment, effective supervision and commitment by management, rather than from technology alone.

Additionally, when properly implemented and enforced, effective waste management can have distinct economic benefits, such as cost saving linked to waste reduction and improved purchasing practices. Such a programme, when supported by committed healthcare management, will contribute to the improvement of patients care, promote health and safety of staff, and help improve the overall economy and operation of the facility. It will also enhance the image of health services with regard to the quality of patient care and protection of the environment.

CONCLUSION

Safe and effective management of waste is not only a legal necessity but also a social responsibility. Lack of concern, motivation, awareness and cost factor are some of the problems faced in the proper hospital waste management. Lack of apathy to the concept of waste management is a major stymie to the practice of waste disposal. The most vital component of the waste management plans that have been formulated is to bring about a transformation in the mind sets and develop a system and culture through education, training and persistent motivation of the health care staff.

The present study aimed to improve the knowledge, attitude and practices towards hospital waste management among the staff through a training programme. The findings of this study confirms that education and training programme increases the knowledge as well as the sense of responsibility resulting in change in attitude and practices. Hence, developing a highly motivated workforce by training in safe practices, monitoring those of practices, with continued improvements would work towards a ***"safe protected biohazard free environment"***

REFERENCES:

1. Dr D B Acharya, Meeta Singh, The text book of hospital waste management, Minerva Press - 2003.
2. Pruss A, Giroult E, Rushbrook P. Safe management of wastes from healthcare activities. Geneva: World Health Organization, 1999.
3. AG Chandrorkar, BS Nagoba, Hospital waste management, 1St Edition, Paras Medical Publisher, 2003.
4. The Ministry of Environment and Forests, Government of India -Bio-medical waste management & handling rules-1998
5. Veda Hegde, Kulkani R D, Ajantha G S –Bio medical waste management .J Oral & Maxillofacial Pathology vol 11 , Issue-1, Jan-June 2007.
6. World Health Organization. Suggested guiding principles and practices for sound management of hazardous hospital waste. New Delhi: Regional Office for South- East Asia, World Health Organization: 3-5, 2000.
7. Treasure E , T Patrick – An Investigation of Disposal Of Hazardous Wastes from New Zealand Dental Practices, CDOE 1997, Vol 25, P 328-331
8. Punchanuwat K, Drummond B K, Treasure E T: An Investigation of disposal of dental clinical waste in Bangkok, International Dental Jouranl 1998, Vol 48, P 369-373.
9. Kishore Jugal, PankajGoel, Sagar.B, T.K.Joshi: Awareness about Biomedical Waste Management and Infection Control among dentist of a Teaching Hospital in New Delhi, India. IJDR 2000, Vol 11, No 4, P 157-161.
10. Darwish RO, Al-Khatib IA. Evaluation of dental waste management in two cities in Palestine. East Mediterr Health J. 2006;12 Suppl 2:S217-22
11. Sudhakar V, Chandrashekar J. Dental health care waste disposal among private dental practices in Bangalore City, India. Int Dent J. 2008 Feb; 58(1):51-4.
12. M. Muhlich, M.Scherrer, F.D.Dascher: comparison of infectious waste management in European hospitals. Journal of hospital infection ,Vol55, issue 4 , Dec-2003, p 260-268
13. Joseph, J, Ajith Krishnan, G.C. (2004) Hospital Waste Management in the Union Territory of Pondicherry – an Exploration. Mahatma Gandhi Dental College and Hospital, Pondicherry
14. Pramukh Swami. Management of bio-medical waste: awareness and practices in a district of Gujarat. Indian J Public Health. 2005 Oct-Dec; 49(4):245-7.
15. Saini.S, S.S.Nagarajan, R.K Sharma :Knowledge, Attitude and Practices of Bio-medical waste management amongst staff of a tertiary level Hospital in India, Journal of the Academy of Hospital 2005, vol 17, No.2

16. Rasheed S, Iqbal S, Baig LA, Mufti K Hospital waste management in the teaching hospitals of Karachi. J Pak Med Assoc. 2005 May; 55(5):192-5
17. Saraf Y, M. Shinde, S.C. Tiwari: Study of awareness status about hospital waste management among personnel and quantification. Indian journal of community medicine 2006, vol 31, no2, p -111
18. Manyele SV, Anicetus H. Management of medical waste in Tanzanian hospitals, Tanzan Health Res Bull. 2006 Sep;8(3):177-82
19. Gupta S, Boojh R. Report: biomedical waste management practices at Balrampur Hospital, Lucknow, India Waste Manag Res. 2006 Dec;24(6):584-91
20. Mohamed Soliman S, Ibrahim Ahmed: A Overview of biomedical waste management in selected Governorates in Egypt: a pilot study. Waste Manag.2007; 27(12):1920-3.
21. Qureshi Waseem MD, Hassan MD; Wani N, Baba MS; SM Kadri MB; Khan Nazir MS Awareness of Biomedical Waste Management amongst Staff of the Government SMHS Hospital, Srinagar A Tertiary Level Hospital in Kashmir Valley. JK- Practitioner January-March 2007 , Vol.14, No. 1,
22. Rao PH. Report: Hospital waste management--awareness and practices: a study of three states in India. Waste Manag Res. 2008 Jun; 26(3):297-303.
23. Abdulla F, Abu Qdais H, Rabi A. Site investigation on medical waste management practices in northern Jordan. Waste Manag. 2008; 28(2):450-8.
24. Bernard Rosner (2000), Fundamentals of Biostatistics, 5th Edition, Duxbury, page 80-240
25. M. Venkataswamy Reddy (2002), Statistics for Mental Health Care Research, NIMHANS publication, INDIA, page 108-144
26. Sunder Rao P S S , Richard J(2006) : An Introduction to Biostatistics, A manual for students in health sciences , New Delhi: Prentice hall of India. 86-160
27. L M Johnnessen Et Al World Bank Working Document – Health Care Wate Management Guidance Note –May 2000.
28. Nazer MW, Pordeus IA, Dental Waste Management in Municipal Health Clinics in Belo Horizonte, Brazil.
29. Pandit NA, Tabish SA, Qadri GJ, Ajaz Mustafa. Biomedical waste management in a Large teaching hospital. JK- Practitioner 2007:Vol.14, No. 1:57-59
30. Sibusiso Derrick Gabela, Health Care Waste Management in Public Clinics in the Ilembe District: A Situational Analysis and Intervention Strategy, November, 2007

QUESTIONNAIRE FOR DENTIST AND DENTAL AUXILLARY

"A STUDY OF KNOWLEDGE, ATTITUDE AND PRACTICE ABOUT HOSPITAL WASTE MANAGEMENT AND TO ASSESS THE EFFECT OF TRAINING AMONG THE STAFF OF DENTAL TEACHING HOSPITALS IN BANGALORE CITY".

Investigator: Dr. Sushma.R.

Dear sir/ madam,

This survey is being conducted as a part of my postgraduate programme to collect the information about hospital waste management. By answering these questions you will be of great help in managing the same, this takes less than 15min of your precious time and please answer all questions in isolation. All the answers will be kept confidential and will not be depicted against your identity.

Thank you.

Name: *Date:*

Age:

Sex: *Male* *Female*

Kindly answer ALL the questions. Tick your answer.

1. Segregation of waste into different categories should be done at

a. The point of generation
b. The time of collection
c. The time of treatment
d. All the above

2. Disinfection before disposal helps to

a. Reduce the risk of transmission of infection.

b. Strengthen and support the overall standards of hospital hygiene

c. Prevents the spread of multidrug- resistant and other nosocomial pathogen.

d. All of the above.

3. Identify the biohazard symbol

a. 

c. 

b. 

d.

4. Which of the following is not an acceptable technique for the handling of sharp needles?

a. Recapping a needle using a cap holder

b. Recapping a needle using a "scoop technique"

c. Disposing of a needle in general trash bag.

d. Disposing of a needle in a puncture –resistant container

5. The presence of personal protective equipments

a. Prevents the transmission of infection from patient to dental health care personnel

b. Prevents the transmission of infection from dental health care personnel to patient.

c. Both of the above

d. None of the above

6. The main risk posed by needle stick injury is exposure of the workers to blood- borne viruses

a. Hepatitis-B (HBV)

b. Hepatitis-C (HCV)

c. Human immunodeficiency virus (HIV)

d. All of the above

7. Infectious waste is given the colour code of

   a. Yellow
   b. Blue
   c. Black
   d. Green

8. Hepatitis-B immunization for health care workers

   a. Not required

   b. May be given.

   c. Compulsory

   d. Any of the above

9. After possible HIV exposure in health care worker

   a. There is no risk of HIV transmission

   b. No immediate measure required

   c. Post exposure prophylaxis to be initiated as soon as possible

   d. None of the above

10. Mercury and excess amalgam should be

    a. Stored in water/ fixer solution

    b. Disposed in general trash

    c. Should be burnt

    d. Should be discharged in waste water.

Please use this scale and tick your answer for each item below

Strongly disagree(SD) ☐ Disagree(D) ☐ don't know (DK) ☐
Agree (A) ☐ Strongly agree(SA) ☐

SD D DK

A SA

11. Segregation of waste at source increases the risk of injury to waste handlers	☐ ☐ ☐ ☐ ☐
12. Decontamination / disinfection reduces chances of infection	☐ ☐ ☐ ☐ ☐
13. Infectious waste should be put in yellow colored plastic bag with bio hazard symbol.	☐ ☐ ☐ ☐ ☐
14.Containment of sharps does not help in safe management of hospital waste	☐ ☐ ☐ ☐ ☐
15.Occupational safety of waste handlers is a must	☐ ☐ ☐ ☐ ☐
16. Reporting of needle stick injury is an extra burden on work.	☐ ☐ ☐ ☐ ☐
17.Use of colour code for segregation of waste is a must	

	☐ ☐ ☐ ☐ ☐
18. Hepatitis-B immunization prevents transmission of hospital acquired infection	☐ ☐ ☐ ☐ ☐
19. Post exposure prophylaxis should be initiated as soon as possible	☐ ☐ ☐ ☐ ☐
20. Excess mercury/ amalgam should be stored in water or fixer solution	☐ ☐ ☐ ☐ ☐
21. Do you segregate waste into different categories at the point of origin?	☐ Yes ☐ No
22. Do you treat sharp waste prior to disposal?	☐ Yes ☐ No
23. Do you dispose infectious waste in yellow colored plastic bag having biohazard symbol	☐ Yes ☐ No
24. Do you use heavy duty (puncture proof) plastic container to collect the waste sharps ?	☐ Yes ☐ No
25. Do you use personal protective devices? • Apron • Mask	☐ Yes ☐ No ☐ Yes ☐ No

• Gloves • Goggles	Yes ☐ No ☐ Yes ☐ No ☐
26. Do you follow system of recording and reporting of injuries/accidents?	☐ Yes ☐ No
27. Do you follow colour code for segregation of waste?	☐ Yes ☐ No
28. Have you taken vaccination against hepatitis B?	☐ Yes ☐ No
29. Following percutaneous exposure do you follow Post exposure prophylaxis?	☐ Yes ☐ No
30. Do you store excess mercury/amalgam in water or fixer solution?	☐ Yes ☐ No

Thank you for your co-operation

<u>ಪ್ರಶ್ನಾವಳಿ</u>

ಆಕ್ಸ್‌ಫರ್ಡ್ ದಂತ ವೈದ್ಯ ಮಹಾವಿದ್ಯಾಲಯ, ಬೆಂಗಳೂರು ನಗರ

ಸಾಮೂಹಿಕ ದಂತ ವೈದ್ಯಶಾಸ್ತ್ರ ವಿಭಾಗ

<u>ಸಂಶೋಧನೆಯ ಶೀರ್ಷಿಕೆ:</u>

ಆಸ್ಪತ್ರೆ ತ್ಯಾಜ್ಯವಸ್ತುಗಳ ನಿರ್ವಹಣೆಯ ಬಗ್ಗೆ ಬೆಂಗಳೂರು ನಗರ ದಂತ ವೈದ್ಯ ಭೋಧನಾ, ಆಸ್ಪತ್ರೆಯ ಸಿಬ್ಬಂದಿಗಳ ತಿಳುವಳಿಕೆ, ಧೋರಣೆ ಮತ್ತು ಅಭ್ಯಾಸದ ಬಗ್ಗೆ ನೀಡಿದ ತರಬೇತಿಯ ಪರಿಣಾಮಗಳು – ಒಂದು ಅಧ್ಯಯನ.

ನಾನು ಡಾ॥ಸುಶ್ಮ.ಆರ್ ಸ್ನಾತಕೋತ್ತರ ವಿದ್ಯಾರ್ಥಿ, ಪ್ರಶ್ನಾವಳಿಯನ್ನು ಉತ್ತರಿಸಲು ನಿಮ್ಮ ಸಹಕಾರ ಕೋರುತ್ತೇನೆ. ಇದರಿಂದ ದೊರೆಯುವ ಮಾಹಿತಿಯು ದಂತ ವೈದ್ಯಕೀಯ ಅನ್ವೇಷಣೆಗೆ ಉಪಯೋಗವಾಗುವುದು.

ವಂದನೆಗಳು

ಹೆಸರು:

ವಯಸ್ಸು:

ದಯಮಾಡಿ ಈ ಎಲ್ಲ ಪ್ರಶ್ನಾವಳಿಯನ್ನು ಉತ್ತರಿಸಿ.

೧. ಬೈಯೋಹೆಜ಼ಾರ್ಡ್ ಚಿಹ್ನೆಯನ್ನು ಗುರುತಿಸಿ

a. 

c. 

b. 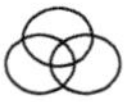

d. 

೨. ಸೋಂಕು ಪೀಡಿತ ತ್ಯಾಜ್ಯ ವಸ್ತುವನ್ನು ಯಾವ ಬಣ್ಣದ ಕಸದ ಡಬ್ಬಿಗೆ ಹಾಕಬೇಕು?

ಅ) ಹಳದಿ ಆ) ನೀಲಿ ಇ) ಕಪ್ಪು ಈ) ಹಸಿರು

೩. ಬಳಸಿ ಎಸೆದ ಸೂಜಿ ಗಾಯಗಳಿಂದ ಯಾವ ರೋಗ ಹರಡುತ್ತೆ?

ಅ) ಹೆಪಟೈಟಿಸ್ ಬಿ ಆ) ಹೆಪಟೈಟಿಸ್ ಸಿ ಇ) ಏಡ್ಸ್ ಈ) ಇವೆಲ್ಲವೂ

೪. ತ್ಯಾಜ್ಯ ವಸ್ತುವಿನ ವಿಲೇವಾರಿ ಮಾಡುವಾಗ ನಿಮ್ಮ ರಕ್ಷಣೆಗೋಸ್ಕರ ಇವುಗಳನ್ನು ಬಳಸಬೇಕು? ಯೂನಿಫ಼ಾರಂ, ಗ್ಲೌಸು, ಮಾಸ್ಕ್	ಹೌದು ☐ ಇಲ್ಲ ☐ ಹೌದು ☐ ಇಲ್ಲ ☐ ಹೌದು ☐ ಇಲ್ಲ ☐
೫. ಬಳಸಿ ಎಸೆಯುವ ಸೂಜಿ ಮತ್ತು ಇತರ ಚೂಪಾದ ಆಯುಧಗಳನ್ನು ಮಾಮೂಲಿ ಕಸದ ಡಬ್ಬಿಗೆ ಹಾಕುವುದು ಸುರಕ್ಷಿತ ವಿಧಾನ?	ಹೌದು ☐ ಇಲ್ಲ ☐
೬. ಆಸ್ಪತ್ರೆಯ ತ್ಯಾಜ್ಯವಸ್ತುವನ್ನು ಅದು ಉತ್ಪತ್ತಿಯಾದ ಸ್ಥಳದಲ್ಲೇ ಬೇರ್ಪಡಿಸುವ ಅಗತ್ಯವಿದೆಯೇ?	ಹೌದು ☐ ಇಲ್ಲ ☐
೭. ತ್ಯಾಜ್ಯವಸ್ತುವನ್ನು ವಿಲೇವಾರಿ ಮಾಡುವಾಗ ನಿಮಗುಂಟಾಗುವ ಗಾಯ ಮತ್ತು ಅಪಘಾತವನ್ನು ವರದಿ ಮಾಡುವುದು ಹೆಚ್ಚಿನ ಕೆಲಸ	ಹೌದು ☐ ಇಲ್ಲ ☐
೮. ಉತ್ಪತ್ತಿಯಾದ ಸ್ಥಳದಲ್ಲಿಯೇ ಬೇರ್ಪಡಿಸುವುದರಿಂದ ತ್ಯಾಜ್ಯವಸ್ತು ವಿಲೇವಾರಿ ಮಾಡುವವರಿಗೆ ಹೆಚ್ಚಿನ ಗಾಯಗಳಾಗುವ ಸಂಭವವಿದೆ.	ಹೌದು ☐ ಇಲ್ಲ ☐
೯. ಆಸ್ಪತ್ರೆಯ ತ್ಯಾಜ್ಯ ವಸ್ತುಗಳಿಂದ ಉಂಟಾಗುವ ಸೋಂಕು ನಿವಾರಣೆಗೆ ಮುಂಜಾಗ್ರತ ಕ್ರಮವಾಗಿ ಚುಚ್ಚು ಮದ್ದನ್ನು (ಹೆಪಟೈಟಿಸ್ ಬಿ) ಪಡೆಯುವ ಅವಶ್ಯಕತೆ ಇದೆಯೇ?	ಹೌದು ☐ ಇಲ್ಲ ☐
೧೦. ಹೆಪಟೈಟಿಸ್ ಬಿ ಚುಚ್ಚು ಮದ್ದಿಂದ ಆಸ್ಪತ್ರೆಯಲ್ಲಿ ಹರಡುವ ಸೋಂಕು ನಿವಾರಣೆಯಾಗುತ್ತದೆ	ಹೌದು ☐ ಇಲ್ಲ ☐
೧೧. ನೀವು ತ್ಯಾಜ್ಯವಸ್ತುವನ್ನು ಉತ್ಪತ್ತಿಯಾದ ಸ್ಥಳದಲ್ಲಿಯೇ ಬೇರ್ಪಡಿಸುವಿರಾ	ಹೌದು ☐ ಇಲ್ಲ ☐
೧೨. ತ್ಯಾಜ್ಯ ವಸ್ತುವಿನ ವಿಲೇವಾರಿ ಮಾಡುವಾಗ ನಿಮ್ಮ ರಕ್ಷಣೆಗೋಸ್ಕರ ಇವುಗಳನ್ನು ಬಳಸುತೀರಾ? ಯೂನಿಫ಼ಾರಂ ಗ್ಲೌಸು, ಮಾಸ್ಕ್	ಹೌದು ☐ ಇಲ್ಲ ☐ ಹೌದು ☐ ಇಲ್ಲ ☐ ಹೌದು ☐ ಇಲ್ಲ ☐
೧೩. ನೀವು ಸೋಂಕು ಪೀಡಿತ ತ್ಯಾಜ್ಯ ವಸ್ತುವನ್ನು ಹಳದಿ ಬಣ್ಣದ ಕಸದ ಡಬ್ಬಿಗೆ ಹಾಕುತ್ತೀರಾ?	ಹೌದು ☐ ಇಲ್ಲ ☐
೧೪. ತ್ಯಾಜ್ಯವಸ್ತುವನ್ನು ವಿಲೇವಾರಿ ಮಾಡುವಾಗ ನಿಮಗುಂಟಾಗುವ ಗಾಯ ಮತ್ತು ಅಪಘಾತವಾದರೆ ಅದನ್ನು ಬರೆದಿಡುವುದೋ ಅಥವಾ ವರದಿ ಮಾಡುವುದೋ ಮಾಡುತೀರಾ?	ಹೌದು ☐ ಇಲ್ಲ ☐
೧೫. ಆಸ್ಪತ್ರೆಯ ತ್ಯಾಜ್ಯ ವಸ್ತುಗಳಿಂದ ಉಂಟಾಗುವ ಸೋಂಕು ನಿವಾರಣೆಗೆ ಮುಂಜಾಗ್ರತ ಕ್ರಮವಾಗಿ(ಹೆಪಟೈಟಿಸ್ ಬಿ) ಚುಚ್ಚು ಮದ್ದನ್ನು ಪಡೆದಿದ್ದೀರಾ?	ಹೌದು ☐ ಇಲ್ಲ ☐